The Cause of Empire

Colonization, Civilization, Extermination - The Echoes That Built Our World

TONY L. SCOTT

Copyright © 2025 by Tony L. Scott. All rights reserved.
ISBN (Hard Cover) - 979-8-9929197-2-1

No part of this book may be reproduced or used in any manner without written permission of the copyright owner except for the use of quotations in a book review.

For more information or permissions, please contact the author:
redeemedwriter718@gmail.com
tlmdscott2@gmail.com

Editor: This book was self-edited by the author.

Book Project Management:
Raindrop Creative, Inc. | StartWrite Publish Team
http://www.raindropbrand.com

DEDICATION

To my beloved grandchildren—Harrison, Rumi, and Mina—
May you always have a godly desire for truth and never be satisfied with convenient stories or comfortable lies. Truth is not opinion. Truth is not an "alternative fact." Truth is not relative to the times or the whims of men. Truth stands on its own, unshaken by culture or power.

To my sons and their spouses—Desmond and Lauren, Mario and Negin—
May you guide your children with courage, teaching them that the Word of God is the foundation upon which we see and understand the world. The Bible is not only the Word of life but the lens through which the beauty and the brokenness of history find their true meaning.

And to my loving and supportive wife, Lisa,
Your unwavering faith and steadfast love have carried me through every page of this work. You are my partner in life, in truth, and in the hope that our family will always seek what is real, what is eternal, and what is grounded in the Word of God.

This book is for you. May it serve as a reminder that truth matters, and that knowing it is the first step in living it.

— "An-Dad" or Papa aka Granddad

"And you will know the truth, and the truth will set you free."
— John 8:32, ESV

Jesus said to him, "I am the way, and the truth, and the life. No one comes to the Father except through me."
— John 14:6

"The sum of your word is truth, and every one of your righteous rules endures forever."
— Psalm 119:160

Table of Contents

Preface 1
Introduction 3

Chapter 1: A Portrait of The Invincible Tribe 5

Chapter 2: Civilization, Colonization, Extermination 7
The Invincible Tribe and the Maroon Legacy 9
The Savagery of So-called Civilization 18

Chapter 3: "Greatness" Built on Genocide and Black Bodies ... 23
The Henry and Hitler Alliances 27
"Indian" Genocide: Stolen Land 28
Blacks as Human Tools and The Construct of Race 33
Sven 35
Dunlop's Rummage for Rubber and the Berlin Conference 35
"The Island of Dr. Moreau" 38
Empire Unmasked: White Mythology 39

Chapter 4: Unsilencing The Past 43
The Fragility of Memory and the Danger of Erasure 49
"Who the 'F' Is Columbus" 50
South America Under Siege 53
De las Casas' Dilemma 54

Chapter 5: The Greatest Unmarked Cemetery in World History ... 59
Enslaved White Children 62
The Weaponization of Words 68
The Haitian Revolution 70
Caged and Commodified 75
Who are We? 78
The Scots-Irish's Violent Ethos: The Confederacy and Birth of the KKK 81

Chapter 6: America: A Nation of Immigrants – A Paradox 85
Teachers of Truth: Howard Zinn and Roxanne Dunbar-Ortiz 89
"Age of Jackson" 91
Jesup: The Embodiment of A Henchman 93

Chapter 7: The Evolution of Mass-Killing 97
European Military Might: "Killing at a Distance" 97
British Execution: A Structure of Violence 100
The Militarization of American Industry 102
The Monroe Doctrine 104
Atomic Destruction: "Dealing With the Animal." 105
Ndugu M'Hali 108
We Are Not a Footnote 110
Heart of Darkness 111

Chapter 8: Muséum National d'Histoire Naturelle 117
Mount Rushmore: A Contradiction 119
Pseudoscience and Survival of the Fittest 122

Chapter 9: Savage, Semi-Civilized and Civilized 127
Institutional Sterility and Racial Erasure 131
Death Mills and Genocide 133
Strategy of Domination 134
Chief Black Kettle and Medicine Woman Ar-no-ho-wok 136
"The Past Has a Future We Never Expect." 138

Chapter 10: The Living and the Dying: We Don't Want to Remember . 141

Chapter 11: "The Bright Colors of Fascism" 151
Land With People: The Myth of Pristine Wilderness 153
Osama bin Laden: "Geronimo" 157
Words Matter: Linguistic Psychology 160
Hunting "Indians" for Pay 162

Chapter 12: The Second Amendment and "The Cult of the Gun" 165
Assault Against So-Called American Exceptionalism 168
Resistance Through Dance 172
General Sherman's Heartless Massacre of Native Peoples 174
The Paradox of Snow 177

Chapter 13: The Real Fight Remains: The Structure of Terror 179
Haiti: Death at Home – How Empire Silences 182
The Assassination of Prime Minister Patrice Lumumba 183
Berlin and Auschwitz Death Camps 183
Rwandan Genocide 184
Charlottesville, Virginia, and Trump: Flawed Leadership 187
The Theater of Nationalism: The Hatred of Others 189
Clash of Civilizations: The Rejected and Despised 190
Peck's Tribute to Sven 195
Renewal and Calling to Account 196

Chapter 14: White Man's Neighborhood - Keep Out 199
"Adolf's Racial Paradise" 201
Genocidal Liquidation 202
20 Minute Walk of Death: "The Banality of Evil" 204
Not Ignorant Brutes 206
Crematorium Blueprint – A Killing Machine 207
"We Still Haven't Seen Anything Yet" 208

Preface

This book was born out of a desire to know more about the cause and effect of history—not just as a collection of dates and events, but as a living, breathing force that continues to shape who we are today. Watching Raoul Peck's *Exterminate All the Brutes* was not merely an encounter with a documentary; it was a confrontation. His work pulled no punches and refused to let myths stand unchallenged. It demanded a response, and this book is mine.

I do not present this work as a scholar or historian but as a student of history and a man of faith. My purpose in writing this book is twofold. First, I want my brothers and sisters in Christ to better understand why the world is the way it is. So much of the conflict, inequality, and division we witness today can be traced back to the systems of colonization and imperialism. These are not abstract ideas; they are historical realities that have had lasting effects on every corner of the globe, including our churches, our communities, and our personal worldviews.

Second, I write this for my grandchildren and future generations—for my offspring who will grow up in a world full of noise, distortion, and competing narratives. I want them to have a reliable source to return to, their grandfather's book, as a point of comparison alongside other trusted sources. I want them to understand the truth of the world they live in, not just what is convenient or commonly told.

My study of the Bible has compelled me to consider history in a broader context. As I seek to understand Scripture, I've been driven to learn more about what has shaped the nations, the people, and the systems we see in place today. The deeper I've gone into history, the clearer it has become that we cannot separate spiritual truth from historical reality.

This book is not a substitute for Raoul Peck's powerful film, but a companion to it. It captures and contextualizes his message, offering additional insight and historical framing for readers who want to explore further.

This is not a comfortable book. It is not meant to be. The stories within it are weighty and, at times, painful. But they are necessary. Because history is not only what happened, but also the story we choose to tell about what happened. And if we choose truthfully, maybe we can walk more wisely in the present and prepare a better way for those yet to come.

— Minister Tony L. Scott

Introduction

History is not dead ink on the pages of dusty books. It is alive. It breathes in the streets we walk; it echoes in the conflicts we witness, and it shapes the world our children will inherit. It is not just the story of the past; it is the foundation of the present.

When I first encountered Raoul Peck's documentary, *Exterminate All the Brutes,* I was struck by its unflinching honesty. Peck tears through the comfortable myths many have come to accept about "civilization," "progress," and "discovery." He exposes the brutality behind those words and forces us to confront what has been deliberately hidden in plain sight. Watching the documentary, I knew that this story could not stay confined to a screen. It needed to be studied, pondered, and placed in the hands of those willing to wrestle with truth.

This book was born from that conviction. It is not merely a retelling of Peck's work, though his powerful narrative is central to its foundation. It is also an expansion—a weaving together of his words, additional historical context, and my own reflections as a student of history. Where Peck presents a visual and emotional journey, this book translates that journey into a form that allows readers to pause, reflect, and dig deeper into the events and ideas that have shaped the world as we know it.

Here, you will find the intertwined stories of colonization, extermination, and resistance. You will see how imperialism did not just redraw maps, but redefined what it meant to be human in the eyes of those who held power. You will trace the threads from the massacres of Indigenous nations in the Americas to the slave ships of the Atlantic, from the plantations and reservations to the death camps of Europe. And you will see that these are not separate histories, but chapters of one continuous story.

This is not a comfortable story to tell. It is not meant to soothe, but to confront. It demands we shed the myths we were taught and face the truth that history is the fruit of power—and that power decides what story gets told.

For students of history, this book serves as a companion to the documentary and a guide through some of the darkest, yet most defining, chapters of human history. For my brothers and sisters in Christ, it is a call to understand the roots of the world's brokenness so that we can better live out our faith with eyes open to truth. And for my grandchildren and those yet to come, this is my offering to you—a record you can return to when the noise of the world becomes loud, a reminder that truth matters, and that understanding the past is the first step toward shaping a just future.

This is not just about what happened. It is about what continues to happen—and what we choose to do with that knowledge.

CHAPTER 1

A Portrait of The Invincible Tribe

The extraordinary and painfully informative documentary *Exterminate All the Brutes,* produced by Raoul Peck, opens with a hauntingly beautiful image: a woman standing solemnly on the screen. She portrays Abby Osceola. Her presence is powerful—her posture proud, her gaze unflinching.

Raoul narrates: "She is from the Seminole Nation. Her story goes deep into the history of this continent." As he speaks, the screen flickers—briefly, almost too quickly to register—with a brutal image of her head being scalped. The violence is not gratuitous; it is historical truth. "She reminds me of my mother," he continues. "But despite the resemblance, they each come—although through not totally unrelated events—from different strands of history."

Then, another image: she is executed at point-blank range by a white soldier.

"It is said that the Seminole Nation never signed any treaty with the United States government. That's why they are called the Invincible Tribe." The Seminole were indeed invincible in spirit and resistance. They never surrendered in the face of forced removal. The First Seminole War (1817–1818), the Second (1835–1842), and the Third (1855–1858) were wars of extermination against a coalition of Native Peoples and escaped African slaves who had made common cause in Florida.

The U.S. government spent more money fighting the Seminoles than it did on the American Revolution itself. General Thomas Jesup, the architect of deceit in that war, once declared, "This is a Negro war, not an Indian war," highlighting the deep racial anxieties and genocidal intentions at play.

But Peck shifts now, as he says: "But for now, it is about another story."

CHAPTER 2

Civilization, Colonization, Extermination

The image in the documentary transitions to a scene of a turbulent ocean, waves crashing beneath a somber sky. The water is dark and unruly, as if haunted. "In that larger story, there are three words that summarize the whole history of humanity: *Civilization. Colonization. Extermination.*"

This trinity of destruction has long defined the march of empire:

- Civilization, used as a mask for conquest.
- Colonization, a process of control, theft, and restructuring of lives.
- Extermination, the inevitable endpoint of a system that sees others not as people, but as obstacles to profit and expansion.

The next image is an open plain, where dozens of buffalo graze peacefully. Peck then adds: "These words run forcibly through Western world history. The same way they drill to the core of U.S. history."

Buffalo were more than food or hide to Native People. They were life. They were sacred. Their near-extinction—engineered by U.S. military policy to starve and subjugate Plains nations—is part of that extermination Peck speaks of. General Philip Sheridan infamously supported the slaughter of millions of buffalo to break Native resistance.

Now provided in the documentary are Native hunters moving in unison with the buffalo. It is a snapshot of balance—a harmony that colonialism was determined to shatter. Peck: "And it is not so much about winners and losers or between conqueror or conquered, nor between colonists and colonized. The forces involved here are less visible than gunfire—class, property, or political crusades—but they are no less powerful."

Black-and-white photographs of Native American families appear—faces worn with history, bodies displaced by policy. "Entire civilizations in the Western Hemisphere were wantonly destroyed, setting the Western world on a path of greed and destruction. For history is the fruit of power, and power is crucial to the story, which then always becomes, at best, a story about who won."

Peck pauses, as though letting the weight of that sentence settle. "And clearly, this needs to be challenged." The screen now shifts to a jarring contrast: white performers dancing and mocking Indigenous people in a stage production. Their gestures are caricatures, their costumes grotesque imitations. Native People are portrayed as savages, animals, and less than human. Superimposed on the screen are the words: On The Town, Gene Kelly, Stanley Donen, 1949.

Hollywood, Broadway, and minstrel stages all participated in the cultural project of dehumanization. Peck lets the performance linger long enough to discomfort the viewer.

"For it is about who we are today. About what we have become as a people. And on what side of history are we on? What side of truth?" Peck's voice sharpens: "A certain view of history contends that the historical narrative is just one fiction among others. It is not. There is no such thing as alternative facts."

The Invincible Tribe and the Maroon Legacy

Appearing now on the screen are the words: Part 1: The Disturbing Confidence of Ignorance.

The camera turns to a dense forest. A place shrouded in silence, alive with memory. Superimposed on the screen are the words: December 1836, Seminole and Maroons Encampment (today's Florida). A history buried beneath the soil. A resistance that echoes still.

Appearing on the other side of the dense forest, standing in an open field, is a female Indian chieftain. She stands still and stoic, staring at the tree line. She utters the words: "This is the day we fight!"

She turns away from the wood line and walks into her village amongst her people. She enters a hut and takes a seat with a few of her Native men, and a couple of Maroons—African men who had escaped slavery and found refuge among the Seminole. These men were part of a growing population known as Black Seminoles.

The term Maroons derives from the Spanish word cimarrón, originally used to describe escaped cattle that fled to the hills and later applied to enslaved Africans who escaped bondage and lived independently in forests and swamps. In the Americas, these self-liberated people formed free communities in defiance of slavery's reach.

Inside the hut, intense and consequential dialogue begins… A Maroon man speaks:

KWAME MIKO: "Chieftain Yah-ho-Cuchee, we must leave. We are the ones who arrived latest here."

YAH-HO-CUCHEE: "Kwame Miko, we are family now. You stay."

KWAME: "Yes. But family is not meant to bring harm."

YAH-HO-CUCHEE: "They bring harm to our nation. Not you."

KWAME: "It's better we surrender, so you and your people can have time to run and hide."

YAH-HO-CUCHEE: "This is our land. The white man wants our land. We fight."

KWAME: "Together. Or we die together."

YAH-HO-CUCHEE: "Hink-lah-mas-tchay." Let's fight!

The scene shifts. Yah-ho-Cuchee and her tribesmen, along with the Maroons, stand side by side, facing the wood line. They pause, waiting, prepared to engage in battle. From the trees emerges Jesup—the "white man"—General Thomas Sidney Jesup, commander of U.S. forces in Florida during the Second Seminole War.

Jesup is known not just for his aggression but for deceit. Under his orders, Native leaders were invited to parley under flags of truce—only to be captured and imprisoned. Jesup saw no distinction between war strategy and treachery.

The documentary shows him stepping forward to address Yah-ho-Cuchee. JESUP: "I do not want to spill Seminole blood, kill Seminole children, Seminole women. Give us back the American property,"—he points to the Maroons—"you stole from our good fellow men, planters, and settlers. And I'll let you move to the Indian Territory, the U.S. government has provided for your people."

YAH-HO-CUCHEE: "You call human beings your property?"

JESUP: "They are slaves."

YAH-HO-CUCHEE: "You steal land. You steal life. You steal humans. What kind of species are you?"

[Jesup draws his gun]

JESUP: "This kind." He fires. Yah-ho-Cuchee is shot in the head. She falls, motionless, to the ground. Her blood stains the soil she vowed to defend. The camera freezes on her lifeless body, then slowly pulls back.

From the woods behind Jesup, a fully armed U.S. military platoon emerges—rifles locked, cannons prepped, some soldiers on horseback, others kneeling in formation. They open fire. Smoke fills the air. Indigenous warriors and Maroons alike fall. Their arrows and muskets are no match for federal firepower. What unfolds is not a battle. It is a slaughter!

Jesup stands unmoved, his face fixed in a defiant yet puzzled expression, as if bewildered that such fierce resistance could come from those he considered subhuman.

This dramatized moment is grounded in historical reality. General Jesup's infamous betrayal of Osceola—whom he captured under a white flag—became symbolic of the United States' broken treaties and brutal expansionist policy. Jesup's insistence that the Seminole surrender the Maroons was a calculated attempt to uphold slavery as the foundation of American wealth and order. But the Seminole refused.

The Maroons and the Seminole were bound not by law or treaty, *but by shared struggle*. Together, they represented a rare and radical solidarity in the face of tyranny. Seminole resistance disrupted slaveholders' profits and challenged the legitimacy of Manifest Destiny. To the white South, this alliance was treasonous. To history, it was heroic.

This was not just a war over land. It was a war over humanity—who would be counted as such, and who would be owned, removed, or erased.

The last shot of the scene lingers on Yah-ho-Cuchee's body—an image of defiance silenced, but not defeated. In the blood of the fallen, a deeper truth is written: liberty, once tasted, will not surrender quietly.

Civilization. Colonization. Extermination. Three words that march in a chilling procession through history! Three words that together form the bloody heartbeat of empire!

We were told that civilization was a gift—that the so-called "civilized world" had a duty, even a divine calling, to spread its culture, language, and religion. But beneath the veil of that mission was a lie—because what they called civilization often meant domination! It meant the erasure of languages, the burning of sacred texts, the breaking of spirits, and the branding of bodies.

Colonization followed close behind, not as a side effect of civilization but as its executioner! It carved up lands as if they were lifeless. It redrew maps with no regard for the people who lived on them. It declared borders with ink and blood. It enslaved, displaced, and re-educated generations into forgetting who they were before the ships came, before the guns came, before the Christian cross was weaponized!

And then came extermination—not always sudden, not always with rifles or gas chambers, but often with silence. With famine as policy. With schools designed to scrub away culture. With diseases unleashed. With prisons that replaced plantations. With the lie, some lives mattered more than others. And when expedient and all else failed, with bullets and boots and bombs.

But perhaps most insidious of all is not just the violence itself, but the disturbing confidence of ignorance that allows it to flourish.

Exterminate All the Brutes shows us this with disturbing clarity. It is the confidence of those who think themselves civilized while building their civilization atop graves. It is the ignorance of history taught in fragments, with colonizers glorified and atrocities buried in footnotes. It is the arrogance that dares to erase the truth while silencing those who dare to speak it.

This confidence is not only historical—it is contemporary. In modern Sweden, the documentary exposes how racism and hate are rising not on the margins but in the mainstream. White nationalism is making itself respectable again. The rhetoric of extermination has returned—this time aimed at Black lives, Jewish lives, immigrant lives. When white populations globally fear that their numbers are dwindling, that others might one day exceed them, the language of "invasion" surfaces.

Immigrants are no longer neighbors or workers or fellow human beings—they are framed as threats. Invaders. Contaminants. And with that framing comes permission to act—to detain, to deport, to dehumanize. And then, it is no surprise when we hear it from the highest office in the land. This madness we are currently seeing in the U.S.

The documentary presents the moment President Donald Trump, at a public rally, refers to immigrants as "animals." Not once. Not in passing. But deliberately. Repeatedly, he has done this. It is not policy debate—it is racialized performance also seen and heard from others outside the U.S. It is state-sponsored language that normalizes cruelty, justifies cages, and whispers to history, "We're still here." Because history is not just something we study.

History is something we repeat when we forget, when we deny, and when we embolden leaders who know exactly what they're doing!

This rhetoric is not new. It is recycled from old regimes, old fears. And it feeds on a kind of panic: the fear of replacement, the fear of white erasure. It's the fear that the "other" is multiplying and that if we don't act now, *they* will take over *our* country. This was the logic of genocide in Rwanda. It was the logic of Hitler's Reich. And now it has found a home in the language of modern democracies—repackaged, televised, tweeted.

As the words "The Dream" appear on the screen, the scene shifts**.** We see and hear President Barack Obama. His speech is not merely patriotic—

it's aspirational. He reminds the nation, "In reaffirming the greatness of our nation, we understand that greatness is never a given. It must be earned." Hence, America's greatness is not a birthright. It is legacy that must be continually justified by our actions as a people. For many, he represents the culmination of centuries of struggle—proof that the arc of the moral universe might, indeed, bend toward justice. His election was the realization of the American Dream. However, for others, it was the beginning of white supremacist backlash.

After Obama's scene fades, the film interlaces the speeches of past presidents—Reagan, Bush, Clinton—and ends with Trump. What we hear in some measure is the evolution of a national myth. I will offer, in one way or another, that each of them, in particularly the Republican presidents, is speaking of America as a *"Shining City On A Hill,"* invoking *Divine Blessing, Manifest Destiny*, and moral superiority. Each leader builds on that myth in their own way—tweaking, modernizing, marketing.

But then comes Trump, who does not aim to expand the dream but to reclaim it. Not for everyone, but for a certain kind of American. A whiter, narrower, meaner America. His chant is not just "Make America Great Again." It's make it like it was before. Before civil rights. Before immigration reform. Before multiracial democracy began to breathe.

Another brief statement of Obama is provided. He says, "We sometimes make mistakes. We have not been perfect. But if you look at the track record, as you say, America was not born as a colonial power."

Raoul offers a rebuttal: "Well, actually, it was. America was born as a colonial power. And this fact is a difficult one to admit, for it bears the fatal capacity to disrupt the core story we have been told all these years and the very foundation of this country. It's not an easy story to tell.

Because the story still continues today. A story of the search for purity and for a godly kingdom. A story of survival and violence. A search for origin, 400 years after the voyage that is said to have made the nation."

The documentary shows us that the dream was always contested. For every voice proclaiming liberty, there was another enforcing bondage! For every speech about equality, there was a policy of exclusion! *The Dream* has always been twofold—one of expansion, and one of control.

And that is the central tension: "Who gets to dream? Who gets to define greatness? Who gets remembered as civilized—and who gets marked for extermination?"

This is where *Exterminate All the Brutes* doesn't just offer a critique. "It issues a challenge! It demands we confront not just what was done, but how we've been trained to see it. It demands we interrogate the myths that soothe us and the lies that empower others. Because *civilization, colonization, and extermination* were never accidents. They were policies! They were ideologies! They were deliberate!"

And until we name them for what they are, and until we confront how they still shape the present, we are doomed to repeat them… this time, not as history, but as news. Because the language of violence begins long before the first shot is fired. The war always starts in the mind. In the pen. On the page. Long before the first slave was shackled, the first land was seized, the first border was drawn—the dehumanization had already begun. The groundwork had already been laid by words that made the inhuman seem natural, even necessary.

Raoul, based on information received from European texts, shares the following: Africans, upon first contact with whites, were not described as people. Not as nations. Not even as tribes. They were referred to as groups. Herds. Species. And worse— beasts.

That was the term used. Beasts. As if Africa were a continent of wildlife, not civilizations. As if the people who lived, loved, worshiped, traded, ruled, and dreamed were no more than animals in the forest, waiting to be subdued, studied, or slaughtered. This was not a fringe view. It was the dominant logic of the European mind during the so-called Age of Discovery—a discovery that always seemed to require someone else's disappearance.

To refer to human beings as beasts is more than an insult. It is a theological declaration. It says you are not made in the image of God. You have no soul that must be respected. You are not redeemable. You are not educable. You are not sovereign. You are expendable. And if you resist, then your resistance is nothing more than animal rage—something to be crushed without remorse. This thinking justified the chain, the whip, the brand, the bullet, the auction block, and the ocean floor.

This ideology did not stay in dusty books. It bled into law. It bled into theology. It was baptized in churches, enforced by soldiers, upheld by courts, and carried in the delusional minds of colonizers who claimed to be saving or civilizing the world.

So when we speak of civilization, colonization, extermination—we are also speaking of classification. A deliberate taxonomy of the human species, where some are lifted and others are listed for removal. The language of "beasts" did not just define the past—it echoes in our present. You hear it when refugees are called swarms. You hear it when protestors are called thugs. You hear it when entire neighborhoods or a people are labeled as infestations. You hear it when a president points to the southern border and says, "These aren't people. These are animals."

And so we must ask: What happens when this language becomes policy? What happens when metaphors become mandates? The doctrine that labeled Africans as beasts never disappeared. It evolved. It became pseudoscience. It became eugenics. It became intelligence tests and redlining, and "stop and frisk." It became immigration quotas and mass incarceration. It became a drone strike that doesn't ask for names. It became a health disparity that doesn't ask why. It became a knee on the neck, while the world watched and debated whether the man beneath it was resisting.

These sordid ideas took sail, but now travel faster than ships, louder than pulpits, more viral than sermons. They live in textbooks, campaign ads, border walls, and algorithms. The "beast" has been rebranded, but never removed. Because extermination doesn't always come with gunfire and violence. Sometimes it comes with forgetting.

That is why *Exterminate All the Brutes* begins not only with images, but with memory. With confrontation. With a refusal to let the silence speak louder than the screams of history. Because what was once written in quiet corners of Europe has now become global noise. And unless we silence the lie, the lie will silence the truth.

The Savagery of So-called Civilization

What was once written in quiet corners of Europe has now become global noise. The lie has been amplified, institutionalized, normalized—no longer confined to books but seared into borders, bodies, and memory.

And that memory is brutal! In one haunting scene, the documentary freezes time on a photograph—two white European men, standing in smug posture beside a severed African head, mounted on a stake. They are not ashamed. They are proud. Their faces are casual, almost bored, as if they were posing beside a deer after a good hunt. But this was no animal. This was a man. A son. Possibly a father. A human being, now reduced to a trophy.

And the horror does not end with the photograph. Because after the shutter clicks and history captures the grinning killers, the body is left behind. The head remains skewered, a warning to the living, a monument to the dead. This is what it meant to resist colonial power. This is what it meant to be labeled beast. Your death would not only be enacted—it would be displayed. And no one would be punished for it. Because the only crime in the eyes of empire was survival.

The documentary does not allow us to look away. It does not sanitize. It refuses to let history wear perfume. Instead, it opens the door to another act of conquest, this time across the Atlantic. The date: May 14, 1607. The place: the banks of what is now Virginia. And the invader: John Smith.

He did not come as a friend, though he may have smiled. He did not come seeking peace, though he spoke the language of diplomacy. He came with entitlement. He came with arms. And he came with a worldview shaped by Europe's long tradition of taking what does not belong to it.

The land he entered belonged to the Powhatan Confederacy, led by Chief Wahunsenacawh, father of the girl we know as Pocahontas. Though the chief extended his hand in peace, offering food, diplomacy, and the hope of coexistence, his trust was betrayed. The English settlers, under Smith's command, seized territory and escalated violence. What began as contact became conquest!

And then, as if to punctuate the savagery of so-called civilization, the documentary shows us a scene that many textbooks will never mention: John Smith scalping a dead Native woman. Not a soldier. Not a warrior. A woman. And not in the chaos of battle, but after death had already come. It is a grotesque act, but it is not random. It is symbolic. It sends a message: You are not safe! Not in life. Not in death. Not in memory.

This was the introduction of European power to the so-called New World. But what wasn't new to the colonizers: the continuation of rape, theft, mutilation, and *the logic of extermination dressed up as discovery.*

The film then takes us back across the ocean, into Europe, to trace the roots of this imperial brutality. It reminds us that these acts were not born on the battlefield but in the ideology of empires that believed themselves chosen. Blessed. Clean.

Enter the Spanish Inquisition, where conquest was not merely military—it was theological. Here, the rulers of Europe began to codify a concept that would haunt the centuries to come: blood purity. Not faith. Not character. Not behavior. Blood.

"Limpieza de sangre"—clean blood—became the test. If your lineage was Christian, Spanish, European—your blood was clean. If you descended from Jews, Muslims, Moors, or Africans, your blood was impure. Dirty. Dangerous. And therefore disposable.

This wasn't science. It was supremacy masquerading as morality. And from this treachery was born a system that would become the scaffolding of white supremacy. Because if blood could be ranked, so could people. If races could be classified, so could rights. And suddenly, the world was no longer full of nations and cultures, but of superiors and subhumans.

Europe's imperial machine took this ideology and ran with it. It set its sights on Africa, Asia, and the Americas—not to learn from them, but to rule over them. Not to admire their civilizations, but to dismantle them. And in every conquest, the myth of clean blood followed. It became the justification for slavery. For rape. For genocide. For apartheid. It said, "We are not just stronger—we are purer. Therefore, we are entitled."

This ideology has never truly died. It has been refined. Sanitized. Mass-produced. It lurks in policies. It lingers in immigration laws. It shows up in neighborhood lines and school curriculums, and sentencing disparities. It can be seen in whose history gets taught—and whose gets buried.

And so the documentary urges us not just to mourn the past but to interrogate the present. Because the logic that placed a severed African head on a stake is the same logic that places migrant children in cages. The same logic that gentrifies neighborhoods while pushing their people out. The same logic that speaks of "great replacement theory" and "white genocide" as if equity were extinction.

Because white supremacy does not need to scream. It only needs to whisper. And it whispers best when it hides behind law, behind nationalism, behind scripture, behind slogans like "Make America Great Again."

But greatness built on genocide is not greatness—it is delusion. It is a lie. And unless we name it, unmask it, and dismantle it, we will continue to inherit its violence, baptize its myths, and hand it down to our children like a sacred heirloom.

CHAPTER 3

"Greatness" Built on Genocide and Black Bodies

But greatness built on genocide is not greatness—it is delusion. It is a myth fortified by blood, maintained by forgetting, and fed to each new generation as pride.

From this delusion rose a doctrine of purity so violent, so enduring, that it consumed not only lands but entire peoples. We see this as we study the Spanish crown, not in its moment of conquest abroad, but in its purges at home. In the name of Christ and Crown, the Spanish expelled the Jews from the Iberian Peninsula. Thousands who had lived there for centuries were now deemed alien, impure, unwanted. Many were tortured, coerced, or forced into false conversions during the Inquisition. But those who clung to their identity were cast out as if they were a disease in need of removal.

And when they were gone, the Muslims were next. Those who had once ruled Spain with flourishing arts, sciences, and architecture—those who helped shape the golden age of Al-Andalus—were now marked for elimination. Some were enslaved. Others fled. And many were slaughtered.

What was once a rich mosaic of cultures was shattered, flattened under the weight of a single fanatical vision: one king, one faith, one blood.

This pattern of expulsion and extermination did not stop in Europe. It was exported to the so-called New World, where the Indigenous Peoples of the Americas faced a similar fate. Their lands were taken! Their gods mocked! Their languages erased! Their bodies enslaved! And when diplomacy failed—or when it was never sincerely tried—they too were killed, displaced, marched into oblivion.

The imperial logic that began in Spain soon spread through Europe like a virus wrapped in flags. And though it took many forms, the seed was always the same: those who are not like us must not live among us. And if they cannot be remade in our image, they must be removed from the earth. This is not hyperbole. This is history.

And so, the documentary brings us face-to-face with its most infamous manifestation: Adolf Hitler. We watch as black-and-white video images are shown—soldiers march, Jews are rounded up, ghettos swell, and execution follows. But Hitler did not invent this violence. He inherited it. He perfected a logic that Europe had been rehearsing for centuries. And he gave it bureaucratic precision.

Through pseudoscience, the Nazi regime justified the unjustifiable. Measurements of skulls. Charts of racial traits. Hierarchies of bloodlines. Jews were declared subhuman. So were Roma people. So were Slavs. So were the disabled. So were the undesirables. The language of beasts returned—only now, dressed in lab coats and PhDs. And Hitler was not alone.

The film forces us to look beyond Europe—to Rwanda, to Cambodia, to Bosnia, to the Congo, to Armenia, to Sudan. It reminds us that genocide is not rare. It is not exceptional. It is a pattern. A method. A project. And it always follows familiar conditions.

In a moment of quiet, the screen presents the phrase: *Conditions of Genocide: Fanaticism. Exploitation. Slavery. Conquest. Contempt for aliens.*

This list is not academic—it is prophetic. It is a warning. Because these are not just the ingredients of history. They are the symptoms of our present. Wherever there is religious zeal without compassion, wherever there is labor extracted without dignity, wherever there are borders drawn to exclude rather than to welcome, wherever people are called aliens, animals, invaders—genocide is not far behind.

And then comes the image that sears itself into the soul: a long table, stretching across the screen, covered in skulls. Hundreds of them. Stacked like trophies. Arranged like cataloged evidence of horror. But these were not artifacts of war. They were the remains of people—mothers, fathers, children. Their lives extinguished, their bodies desecrated, their skulls displayed by the very forces that claimed to bring order, progress, and civilization.

It is in this moment that the myth is shattered completely. Civilization is not the opposite of savagery—it is often its mask.

And then the film returns, almost as if to hammer the final nail, to Hitler, standing before a roaring crowd. He raises his voice and declares with terrifying certainty: "The result of this war will be the complete annihilation of the Jewish race in Europe."

Not defeat. Not deportation. Annihilation!

It is a vision rooted not only in hatred but in confidence—the same confidence that once described Africans as beasts, that classified bloodlines in Spain, that scalped Native women on American soil, that photographed severed heads, and that now finds expression in rhetoric, in borders, in silence.

Because the truth is this: genocide does not begin with bullets. It begins with words. It begins with indifference. It begins with the belief that some lives do not matter, or that some people are a problem to be solved.

And unless we confront that belief—wherever it lives, in whatever form—it will continue its march. Not just through history books. But through our world. Even so, it is this belief that shaped not only empires, but the man whose name still casts a shadow over the modern world: Adolf Hitler.

The documentary peels back the mythology to reveal the boy behind the dictator. A child formed in the cultural soil of European supremacy. He did not invent the idea of conquest—he inherited it. As a young man, Hitler studied the histories of empire. And what he saw was not condemnation, but celebration. He saw how European powers had taken whole continents—Africa, Asia, the Americas—and declared them empty, undeveloped, unclaimed, despite the thriving civilizations that lived there for millennia.

He watched how Britain carved up India, how Belgium ravaged the Congo, how Spain and Portugal divided the globe like spoils at a feast. He took notes. And he no doubt internalized the logic: If they could do it, why not Germany? If the British could slaughter and still be called civilized, if the Americans could displace Native Peoples and still be called democratic, then why couldn't he expand his own empire eastward into Slavic lands? Why couldn't he eliminate what he saw as obstacles to purity and progress?

Hitler took his cues not from barbarians, but from imperialists. And he was not alone.

The Henry and Hitler Alliances

Among those who admired and aided him, Henry Ford—the American industrialist—stands as a chilling example. Ford did more than build cars. He published antisemitic propaganda, including The International Jew, a series of writings so vile that Hitler kept Ford's portrait on his wall. The admiration was mutual. Ford's ideology fed Hitler's vision, and Hitler's crimes were carried out in a world that too often remained silent.

Then appears footage, where a large United States flag is shown side by side with an equally large Nazi swastika, affixed to the front entrance of the Grand Central Palace. Occurring at this location was the German American Bund rally, 1937. This image signals the ideological alignment and a pro-Nazi message wrapped in American nationalism. Furthermore, this image reminds us that white supremacy and fascism were not foreign to America, but had institutional footholds within U.S. society.

The documentary makes it clear: Hitler was not an aberration. He was a product. A product of centuries of conquest, pseudoscience, nationalism, and racial hierarchy. And while some spoke out, far too many were silent. Their silence was not passive—it was permission. It was complicity.

From there, the documentary pans outward—from Europe to the global sweep of imperialism. The violent hunger of empire was not limited to one man, one country, or one time. It was a doctrine that stretched across oceans, under many flags. British. French. Dutch. Spanish. Portuguese. German. Belgian. American.

"Indian" Genocide: Stolen Land

Explorers—glorified in textbooks and cast in bronze—were, in truth, the scouts of empire. Men like Columbus, Cortés, de Soto, Cartier, and Cabot did not "discover" anything. They arrived on already-inhabited lands and claimed them in the name of distant kings. They carried crosses and cannons. They planted flags where children had already been born. They redrew maps as if no one else lived there.

This is what the documentary identifies as settler colonialism. Not just colonization from afar, but invasion with the intent to stay. To settle. To possess. It was not merely about trade or resources—it was about land. And land, to the settler, meant opportunity. But to gain that opportunity, someone else had to lose everything.

The documentary details how settler colonialism in the Americas became a calculated machine of displacement and death. The land was advertised with glowing terms—"Indian Territory, Garden of the World, open for settlement." But such settlement required the elimination of the Native People.

One advertisement reads like a real estate pitch, but it drips with genocide: "Indian land for sale. Get a home of your own. Easy payment. Perfect title. Possession within 30 days."

As if the land were vacant. As if it hadn't been cultivated, prayed over, fought for, lived in. As if homes, sacred grounds, and burial sites could be wiped clean with the stroke of a pen and the swing of a rifle.

Other ads boast of land in the West—"irrigated, irrigable, agricultural, fertile." Land of promise, sold cheap, sold fast, sold to the dreamers of manifest destiny. But that dream was someone else's nightmare.

To make it possible, the Native People had to be made invisible, or removed altogether. Treaties were broken. Reservations imposed. Schools built to erase language and memory. And where persuasion failed, violence answered. Settler colonialism was not an accident. It was a program. It was a campaign of permanent occupation—and permanent removal.

This, the documentary insists, is the legacy we inherit. This is not a wound of the past. It is a scar that still burns. Because the mindset of entitlement—the belief that some are meant to own and others to be owned—has never fully died. It has changed its language, shifted its borders, updated its tools. But the engine still runs.

And that engine, unchecked, leads always to the same place: a land cleared not by law, but by blood. A land gained not by courage, but by conquest. A history built not on liberty, but on the erasure of those who were here long before the first settler dreamed of home.

This, the documentary insists, is the legacy we inherit. This is not a wound of the past. It is a scar that still burns. Because the mindset of entitlement—the belief that some are meant to own and others to be owned—has never fully died. It has changed its language, shifted its borders, updated its tools. But the engine still runs.

That engine was fed not only by bullets and policies, but by advertisements, pieces of paper that sold death with a smile. "Indian Land for Sale," another poster reads, "Inherited land. Perfect for settlers."

As if injustice could be inherited like property. As if massacre could be passed down like a family heirloom. As if the blood that fertilized the soil came with no obligation—only opportunity.

Another placard beckons: "Come to Northern Kansas. Bring your family." No mention of the families already there. No mention of the treaties torn apart. Just a bright invitation to settle on someone else's grave.

The documentary then presents a chilling visual—a graphic map of North America beginning in 1782, the land shaded in its original form, sovereign, Indigenous, unceded. But as the years tick forward—1782… 1804… 1830… 1850… 1882—we watch the land change color. Not slowly. Not passively. But rapidly, violently. The territory claimed by European settlers spreads like an infection, consuming everything in its path.

By the end of the animation, nearly all of what we now call the United States of America is shaded, claimed, conquered, and renamed. The Native presence has been pushed to the margins or erased entirely. This is not migration. It is not settlement. It is systematic removal and extermination!

Then comes the voice of Raoul Peck, who indicts America by offering that this nation has not acknowledged that it has committed genocide, an evil that it refuses to own.

This is not a metaphor. It is not hyperbole. It is the truth of history calling to a nation that has yet to fully confess. Because genocide is not just about killing. It is about erasure—of land, of language, of lineage, of memory.

And even today, whether subconsciously or consciously, Native Americans continue to face violence, oppression, and discrimination. Not in the past, but in the twenty-first century. In land rights. In health care. In police violence. In voter suppression. In broken treaties that still sit unsigned or unhonored. The settler project did not end—it evolved. And Native existence is still treated as resistance.

Then, in one of the most haunting images in the documentary, the camera lingers on photographs of Native American children. Hundreds of them. Lined up. Silent. Dressed not in their traditional garments but in stiff European clothing—buttoned collars, tight shoes, forced conformity. They are standing in rows outside of the Carlisle Indian Industrial School in Pennsylvania, one of many institutions designed not to educate, but to indoctrinate.

Here, the motto was explicit: "Kill the Indian, save the man."

At Carlisle, Native culture was not respected. It was erased. Children were forbidden from speaking their languages, practicing their customs, or seeing their families. Their hair was cut. Their names were changed. Their spirits were broken. What the rifle had not accomplished, the classroom would finish.

This was not education—it was assimilation by force. A quiet genocide aimed not at bodies but at identity. And its effects are still felt in generations of trauma, cultural dislocation, and spiritual loss. These children were not lost. They were taken, forced to conform. And the photos, as they sit frozen in time, speak louder than any textbook. They say: We were here. We were changed. But we remember. Because memory cannot be colonized.

And so, the documentary presses us again—not to pity, not to guilt—but to confront. To reckon. To refuse the lie that the past is past. Because the past is present. And if we do not challenge the foundations, we will continue to build America's empire on top of the same bones.

But even memory must contend with the blood that stains the soil.

Exterminate All the Brutes presses deeper into the truth that settlement did not come peacefully. The myth of noble settlers and passive tribes is shattered. The documentary reminds us that many Native Peoples did not give up their land without a fight. They resisted—not out of savagery, but out of sovereignty. They fought not because they were violent, but because they were defending what was sacred: their homelands, their ancestors, their right to exist without chains or exile.

And so, violence erupted—not just upon the Native Peoples, but upon the settlers who came to take what was not theirs. Blood was shed on both sides, but only one side came looking for war. Only one side arrived with entitlement wrapped in scripture and rifles. The other side was trying to survive.

But in the logic of empire, resistance is always framed as aggression.

And so, the violence was used as further justification: "See? These people are savage. They cannot be reasoned with." And thus, the machinery of extermination moved forward, cloaked in the language of progress.

With resistance crushed and treaties broken, the land was no longer treated as sacred. It became real estate. Commoditized. Measured. Mapped. Divided. Sold. Not to the Native Peoples who had cared for it for generations, but to the very people who had taken it by force.

Land became wealth, but only for the invaders. To the settler's mind, land was not spiritual. It was financial. It was a resource to be extracted, not a relationship to be honored. The sacred mountains became mining claims. The rivers became property lines. The forests became currency. But land alone was not enough to build empire. To extract wealth from the land, they needed labor. And so, they brought it in chains.

Blacks as Human Tools and The Construct of Race

The enslavement of Africans became the backbone of this new economy. Black bodies were bought, sold, whipped, worked, raped, and bred—not as humans, but as tools. The wealth of the Americas—its cotton, its sugar, its tobacco, its railroads, its buildings—was built by those who were never meant to enjoy it.

But there was a problem for the empire: the oppressed were many. And if poor white indentured servants and enslaved Africans found common cause, they might rise together. And so, the colonial powers introduced a new invention—race.

For the first time in human history, a caste system was created not by religion, not by tribe, not even by wealth, but by skin color. White poor people were told they were superior to Black people, not because of merit, but because of melanin. And that lie stuck.

White indentured servants, many of whom had been treated only slightly better than slaves themselves, were granted privileges—land, legal protections, social status—on one condition: they had to see themselves as white first, and human second.

And the enslaved Africans? They were dehumanized entirely. Treated as chattel. Given no name, no right, no identity. Race became the dividing wall that ensured that the oppressed would never unite. This was not accidental. It was strategic. Divide the poor. Elevate whiteness. Protect power. And while this system crushed Black life and broke white solidarity, it also desecrated the land, again and again.

The land, which was seen as sacred by the Indians, now became desecrated by *the land thieves.*

The land was not just taken—it was defiled. Its sacred places mined. Its animals hunted to extinction. Its waters poisoned! Its people displaced! What had once been lived with was now lived on top of. What had once been revered was now exploited.

And so, the land itself testifies. It bears witness to the blood. To the bones. To the treaties that lie buried beneath suburbs and highways. It remembers what the textbooks forget. And the question remains: how long will we pretend that theft is discovery… That destruction is destiny… That desecration is development?

Because until that lie is broken, the land will remain soaked with the silence of those who will not name the truth.

Sven

It is in that same spirit of naming—of remembering and resisting erasure—that Raoul Peck opens up a deeply personal moment in the documentary. He speaks of his friend and fellow truth-teller, the Swedish author Sven Lindqvist—whose words helped shape the very foundation of this film. Sven, a white European, did not flinch in the face of his own people's legacy. He did not distance himself from history. He walked straight into it.

Raoul speaks with tenderness and reverence about their friendship—how Sven, through his writings and his lived convictions, bore witness to the horrors of white imperialist power. And yet, their bond was not built on guilt or performance—but on truth, on integrity, on mutual human dignity.

This, Raoul reflects, should not be the exception. The image of a white man and a Black man walking side by side through history—not in denial or defensiveness, but in shared witness—this should be the rule. This should be how we remake the world.

And then, as if to underscore the stakes of that friendship, the documentary plunges us back into the brutal consequences of unchecked empire. It introduces what Raoul titles "The Murky Secret Of Rubber."

Dunlop's Rummage for Rubber and the Berlin Conference

At the center of this chapter is a Scottish surgeon and inventor named John Boyd Dunlop, who in the late 19th century created and patented the inflatable rubber tire, initially to ease the bike rides of his sickly son. What seems at first like a tale of innovation quickly becomes a window into exploitation and rummage for rubber.

Because just four years earlier, the Berlin Conference of 1884–85—often sanitized in textbooks as the Congo aka Berlin Conference —had already drawn up the roadmap for European plunder of Africa. In quiet rooms in Berlin, without a single African present, the European powers—Belgium, France, Britain, Portugal, Germany—carved the continent into zones of control. Not based on tribal lands, not based on cultural ties, not based on any respect for sovereignty—but based purely on imperial appetite.

Rubber, they had discovered, would be gold. And Africa would be the mine. The colonial mindset was simple and vicious: take the land, loot the resources, dominate the people—by any means necessary! Deception, violence, forced labor, religious manipulation, scorched-earth tactics—nothing was off limits. This was not partnership. It was pillage.

Dunlop's tire would roll on roads paved in Congolese blood!

Rubber wasn't the only thing taken. So too was the autonomy of Africa. Self-governance was shattered, societies dismembered, traditions suppressed. And the effects of that disruption are not merely historical—they are contemporary, felt across the continent to this very day in poverty, instability, underdevelopment, and fractured political structures.

No European figure embodies this brutal theft more than King Leopold II of Belgium. The documentary pulls no punches! Under the mask of philanthropy and "civilizing mission," Leopold seized the entire Congo Free State as his personal possession—not a colony of Belgium, but his private fiefdom. And from that fiefdom, he plundered rubber and ivory—and most horrifically, bodies.

Africans were worked to death, forced to meet rubber quotas under threat of mutilation, execution, and destruction. Villages were burned to the ground. Children were taken as hostages. Hands were chopped off—not just as punishment, but as proof that bullets had not been wasted. Failure to comply was met with terror.

This was not empire. This was a multibillion-dollar heist!

And the profits were staggering. The wealth sucked out of the Congo flowed into Belgium, materializing in luxurious buildings, grand avenues, and imperial monuments in Brussels—monuments that still stand, paid for by Congolese pain.

And what did the world know of this? Very little—until a sailor turned writer began to take note. Enter Joseph Conrad, who served as a captain on a steamboat in the Congo. What he saw at the trading posts, what he heard in hushed conversations, what he witnessed in the depths of the jungle—left him shaken. The horrors did not match the myths. The civilization he had been promised was nowhere to be found. What he saw was madness. Greed. Murder disguised as trade.

His short novel, Heart of Darkness, attempts to capture the soul-rotting brutality of colonial ambition. But even Conrad, despite his insight, was still a man of his time—his gaze limited, his language haunted by the same racial hierarchies he tried to expose. Still, his words cut deep, because he saw what many refused to see: the real darkness was not in the jungle—*it was in the heart of the empire itself.*

And so, rubber became not just a material—but a metaphor. A symbol of everything empire promised and everything it destroyed. A child's tire became a noose for a continent. And the profits rolled in, while the bodies piled up.

The murky secret of rubber is not just about a product, it's about how easily we consume without conscience, how violence becomes invisible when it's turned into wealth, and how empire always finds a way to justify itself—until someone tells the truth.

That is precisely what Joseph Conrad tried to do—though bound by the blinders of his time. And he was not alone. Another literary mind, H.G. Wells, shared this struggle—two writers wrestling with the age of empire, trying to make sense of civilization's madness.

"The Island of Dr. Moreau"

In The Island of Dr. Moreau, Wells gives us a twisted metaphor for empire. The novel centers on a scientist, Dr. Moreau, who conducts grotesque experiments on "animals" trying to "civilize" them into human beings. They are taught language. They are forced into clothes. They are beaten into submission. But they never stop being animals in the doctor's eyes. Their humanity is conditional, fragile, revocable.

This is not just fiction. This is imperial ideology reimagined. The story speaks to the notion of the "civilized savage"—a term soaked in contradiction. The colonizer sees himself as godlike, a bringer of order and knowledge, reshaping beasts into men. But the effort is never sincere. The goal is not elevation, it is control.

In one haunting moment, Dr. Moreau declares, "Do you know what it means to feel like God?" The line drips with arrogance, with the hubris of conquest. This is the very feeling that undergirded colonial domination:

the illusion of superiority, the intoxication of reshaping the world through domination and violence.

Peck shows us that the narrative of civilization was never meant to uplift the colonized. It was a performance, a violent act cloaked in benevolence. And fiction—whether by Conrad or Wells—offered a mirror to empire, even when it couldn't fully name its own reflection.

From literature, the documentary shifts to cinema, and with it, the power of image to reinforce—or resist—imperial mythology.

Empire Unmasked: White Mythology

Raoul draws from Francis Ford Coppola's 1979 masterpiece, Apocalypse Now, a film that transposes Heart of Darkness from colonial Congo to the Vietnam War. The jungle is still present. So is madness. So is the god complex of white military men far removed from consequence.

The film's most iconic scenes—the napalm engulfing villages, the helicopter raids set to Wagner, the descent into moral anarchy—are not simply about Vietnam. They are about the logic of empire itself: *when you declare yourself a civilizing force, you authorize every atrocity in the name of peace.* Peck is not using these clips to critique Coppola—but to amplify the emotional and philosophical thread that connects modern warfare to colonial conquest.

Then, a new scene appears on the screen: Werner Herzog's Aguirre, The Wrath of God (1972). A different continent. A different madness. This time, a Spanish conquistador descends into delusion in search of El Dorado. What begins as a mission becomes a fever dream. What begins as conquest ends in isolation and death.

Raoul doesn't use this film for entertainment—he uses it to expose the psyche of the imperialist. Aguirre, much like Leopold, believes he is ordained to rule. But as the river swallows his men and his mission, we are left with the haunting image of a single man ranting to monkeys, claiming to be the king of nothing. This is empire unmasked: *delusion, destruction, and death*.

And then, as if to draw the cultural mythology full circle, Raoul brings us to the cinematic idol of empire: Tarzan.

In the final scene of Part 1, we are shown David Yates's The Legend of Tarzan (2016). A white man, born of aristocracy, raised by apes in Africa, returns to the continent not only to reclaim his legacy—but to "save" the Native People. This fantasy is no accident. It is the culmination of white mythology. A narrative where whiteness is not only central—it is savior. Africa is still wild, still dark, still waiting to be tamed. And the one who does the taming, the one who swings through the trees with perfect instinct, is not African—but European.

Raoul Peck doesn't need to spell it out. The symbolism speaks volumes. This is the colonial imagination preserved through pop culture: the white body as noble, the Black body as backdrop, and the land as playground.

But then comes the final blow. As the documentary draws to a close, it shifts from fiction back to reality. We are shown photographs—not staged, not scripted, but real. White men groping Indigenous children and women, their eyes vacant, their power unchecked. These are not isolated incidents. They are the outgrowth of an entire ideology: that whiteness confers permission, that might makes right, that the colonized body is an object to be taken, displayed, and violated.

The film closes Part 1 with a devastating confession: *"White—by birth. A default setting."*

That is the unspoken truth beneath centuries of conquest. Not superiority by merit. But privilege by default. The starting point of whiteness is not innocence, but inherited advantage. And with that advantage came silence, complicity, and violence.

And then, finally, Raoul Peck gives us this truth: **"The happiness of one cannot be built on the pain of others."**

It's not just a moral observation—it is an indictment of the entire colonial project. A happiness that rests on stolen land, stolen labor, and stolen bodies is not happiness at all. It is illusion. It is theft sanctified by law, by scripture, by art, by silence.

To ease the guilt, to justify the brutality, the colonizers drew cartoons. They invented caricatures of Africans—"'brutes,' 'beasts,' ' savages"— depicting them abducting white women, murdering white men, attacking so-called civilization. These images were not based on truth—they were based on fear and projection. A way to make violence seem necessary. A way to make genocide look like justice.

- These were not just drawings. They were weapons. And they worked.
- Because if the African is a brute, then the whip is mercy.
- If the Native is a savage, then the bullet is salvation.
- If the Other is not fully human, then nothing done to them can ever be called evil.

This is how history was rewritten—not with facts, but with fictions powerful enough to build nations upon.

And that is where Part 1 leaves us—not with closure, but with confrontation. What do we do with a history built on lies? What do we do with a truth that's been buried beneath monuments and myths?

We unearth it! We name it! We refuse to look away! Because the future we deserve cannot continue to be built on the pain we refuse to see!

CHAPTER 4

Unsilencing The Past

Part 2 of the documentary opens not with narration, but with a single line across the screen: "Ahatti, 1492." A name—Haiti—before it was renamed, rewritten, redefined.

We are shown a group of Native Islanders—a people of color, standing along the shore, watching as a small boat of five European explorers—colonizers, row toward the island. Among them is a priest, dressed in his garb, cross around his neck, a Bible in hand, representing not just religion, but the weaponization of faith in the service of conquest.

They step onto the sand with audacity. Claiming the land as their own. Giving thanks to God for something that was never theirs to begin with. Their piety is performance. Their gratitude is theft in robes. They act as though the presence of the cross absolves the taking of the land.

As the explorers are approached by the curious Native People, suspicion rises—not among the islanders, but among the colonizers. Suspicion turns to fear. Fear turns to violence. And violence turns back on them.

In this imagined encounter—or perhaps one among many historical confrontations—the colonizers lose their lives. Now, whether this scene emerges from the documented past or from Raoul Peck's narrative imagination, it rings with historical truth. There must have been instances like this—moments of resistance, moments where curiosity clashed with conquest, and where the colonizer's arrogance proved fatal.

But the response to that resistance was never peace.

The scene shifts, suddenly, ominously—to a fleet of ships, dozens deep, appearing on the horizon like a plague. What began as five men with a priest becomes the full weight of empire: a swarm of sails, cannons, bodies, muskets. The invasion is no longer speculative. It is systemic. Calculated. Ruthless!

And then—without explanation—we are in a new time, a new place. The screen reads: "Port-au-Prince, Haiti. 1960."

We are no longer watching empire from above. We are inside it. Inside Raoul Peck's own memory, as he recounts the early contours of his childhood in Haiti. What begins as autobiography quickly reveals itself to be autobiography shaped by empire—intimate, and yet global.

He recalls the last page of his kindergarten reading book, and the image that remained with him: An allegorical depiction of Saint Francis of Assisi, a white man, serene, pious, holy—the image of sanctity printed in a textbook on a colonized island.

What does it mean for a Black Haitian child to have whiteness as his introduction to holiness?

What does it mean for colonialism to not just seize the land, but the symbols, the scriptures, the self-proclaimed faces of God? Saint Francis stands at the crossroads of memory and indoctrination—a reminder that colonialism does not only conquer with weapons, but with pictures, icons, and European saints.

And then, the childhood memory turns violent!

Raoul recounts a moment—still vivid decades later—when he got into a schoolyard fight with another student. It seemed, as all school fights are, a petty matter. Something to be resolved with stern words, handshakes, and then moving on. He was sent to the office of the school priest at the Jesuit Institute Primary School. He expected discipline in the form of correction, perhaps repentance. But what he received was pain!

Without a word, the priest struck him… three times! Then he struck the other boy… three times!

Not words. Not grace. Not reconciliation. Violence—institutional, unexpected, unexplained. Raoul says the pain left his tender body raw. But even worse, it left his soul stunned. So stunned, in fact, that he could not cry. He could not understand what had happened to him, only that something had shattered.

That moment—on that day in a Catholic school on an island first colonized in 1492—became a breaking point. He walks out into the schoolyard, alone. And as he stands there, he begins to realize that something he had always assumed—about order, about justice, about faith, was no longer true. His innocence did not dissolve in stages. It was ripped from him.

And in that rupture, his faith in God began to falter. Not because of doubt, but because of betrayal. Not because he stopped believing in good, but because the agent of what should have been good had become the agent of pain and brutality. This, too, is colonization. Not just in ships. Not just in borders. But in the heart of a child, taught to trust the system, only to find that the system bore the hand that struck him.

That blow was more than punishment. It was the extension of a logic that began in 1492—the same logic that claimed land by the cross, enslaved by the gospel, and punished Black bodies in the name of salvation. That moment, that loss of innocence, became Raoul Peck's first awakening to a truth he would spend his life uncovering.

And so, Part 2 of the documentary does not open with statistics. It opens with a scar—in history, and on the body. *Because empire doesn't just reshape the world. It reshapes the soul.*

The screen shifts—bold, defiant, direct: "Who the 'F' is Columbus?" That's not just a question. That's a reckoning.

It is here that Raoul Peck opens this section of the documentary not with rage, but with reverence. He recalls Michael-Rolph Trouillot, a brilliant Haitian scholar whose sudden death left a void in the world of post-colonial thought. Peck names him with love, admiration, and profound gratitude—not only as a friend, but as a guide. A thinker whose work tore through the lies of empire and gave language to truths buried beneath centuries of silence.

He speaks specifically of Trouillot's book, "Silencing the Past," a transformative work that reveals how history is not what happened, but what is told, who tells it, and who is silenced in the process. The past, as Trouillot argues, is often edited—not by accident, but by design. And nowhere is that design more apparent than in the Western narrative of exploration, conquest, and heroic empire.

That is why the question **"Who the 'F' is Columbus?"** matters.

Because for generations, the answer was scripted in textbooks: brave explorer, bringer of civilization, founder of the New World. But the truth—known and documented—is that Columbus was a colonizer, a slave trader, and a butcher. He didn't discover a new world. He invaded an old one. He didn't civilize a people. He enslaved them! Raped them! Sold children into bondage! Initiated genocide!

Raoul's invocation of Trouillot is more than tribute. It's a declaration: We will no longer let the empire write the only version of events. And with that, the film pivots—from the shores of the Caribbean to the dusty plains of Texas. On screen appears the next title: "The Alamo." A symbol of American patriotism. A shrine to frontier bravery. A Hollywood legend.

Raoul reminds us of the iconic film The Alamo, starring John Wayne—that great myth-maker of the American West. He reminds us, again invoking Trouillot's wisdom, that "history can be selected." And in the case of The Alamo, it has been. The American retelling paints a picture of underdog heroism—brave white settlers making a last stand against the tyrannical Mexican army. But history, actual history, tells a different story.

Enter General Antonio López de Santa Anna. In whitewashed retellings—especially in American cinema—Santa Anna is depicted as the villain: brutal, arrogant, tyrannical. But in truth, he was the president of Mexico defending his sovereign nation against *illegal American settlers*, many of whom had brought slavery into Mexican territory, violating the country's laws.

You see, Mexico had abolished slavery in 1829—a fact often erased from the story. When Santa Anna and his troops arrived in Texas (then a part of Mexico), they weren't launching an unprovoked invasion. They were trying to expel colonizers who had settled illegally and refused to follow Mexican law, including the law banning slavery.

The Battle of the Alamo, therefore, wasn't about liberty. It was about the preservation of white domination, land theft, and slaveholding in defiance of Mexican sovereignty. William B. Travis, James Bowie, and Davy Crockett weren't freedom fighters—*they were occupiers.*

General Santa Anna's attack was not tyranny—it was enforcement. But through cinema, through textbooks, through monuments, the story was inverted. The slaveholders became heroes. The law became oppression. The Mexican general became a caricature who stood in the way of the white man's so-called divine destiny.

And so Raoul Peck asks us to consider: Who controls the narrative? Who gets to be remembered as a hero? Whose brutality is forgiven, and whose resistance is criminalized? This is not about nostalgia. It is about power. Because when a lie is told long enough, with enough confidence, and on enough movie screens, it becomes memory. And memory becomes identity. And identity becomes politics.

This is how empires preserve themselves: Not just with guns. But with stories. And so, we return to Trouillot. We return to Peck's challenge. To unsilence the past. To reject the script. To tell the truth—even when it shatters what we thought we knew.

Because when Columbus is a hero, and Santa Anna is a villain, when Tarzan is king, and Africans are brutes, when the Alamo is sacred, but Haiti is forgotten—we are not watching history. We are watching propaganda.

The Fragility of Memory and the Danger of Erasure

The scene shows on the screen, "Berlin, Germany. The Shoah Memorial." Not just a monument. A warning. A sacred space carved into silence, where grey slabs rise like graves and cast long shadows over our collective amnesia. A place designed to disorient, to evoke the very terror and isolation that so many felt—but could not escape. A space where the memory of genocide refuses to rest.

And it's here that Raoul Peck, standing amidst this memory-scape, asks a question that shocks not because it's obscene, but because it's necessary in a world where denial thrives: "Does it matter if the Holocaust is true or false?" "Does it matter if the killing of millions of Jews is relevant or not?"

He doesn't ask because he doubts. He asks because so many others now do. In a world awash with revisionism, conspiracy, and manufactured ignorance, he is exposing the fragility of memory and the danger of erasure. And so—yes, it matters. It matters because truth must never be optional. Because the Shoah is not a footnote. It is a rupture. It is the consequence of dehumanization taken to its full, industrial conclusion.

And yet Peck is not only asking whether the Holocaust is real. He is asking—why do some genocides get memorials while others are buried under silence and denial? Why is this atrocity mourned, while the genocide of the Congo, of Indigenous Americans, of Haitians under Columbus, is rationalized—or worse, forgotten?

And then, the screen shows a name. "John Berkut, deported in February 1944, at the age of four." One child. One date. One deportation—too early to understand, too late to be saved.

Raoul asks again, piercing deeper: "Does it matter the number of Jews murdered?" "Is one count versus another of any real consideration or consequence?" He isn't just talking about the Holocaust. He's laying bare the moral rot at the heart of every society that plays arithmetic with atrocity. Because every number is a name. Every name is a person. And every life deserves memory.

But history—especially when controlled by empire—picks its martyrs and silences the rest. It calculates worth by proximity to whiteness. And in that ledger, Indigenous non-white people, African, and colonized bodies are often left uncounted.

This is the truth *Exterminate All the Brutes* demands we face: Before the Shoah, before Auschwitz, before the gas chambers, there was a longer, older story. One that began not in 20th-century Europe, but in 1492.

"Who the 'F' Is Columbus"

It is here that Raoul turns his attention back to the myth of Christopher Columbus. The man exalted in schoolbooks and statues. The man whose name adorns boulevards, parades, and national holidays. The so-called "discoverer" of a land that had never been lost. But Columbus did not bring civilization. He brought genocide. He didn't chart a New World. He unleashed a new system of domination—one backed not only by sword, but by Scripture.

That's why the numbers matter. That's why the names matter. Because when history becomes selective, genocide becomes negotiable. And when genocide is negotiable, no one is safe!

Raoul reminds us that Columbus did not set out to find the Americas. He was seeking the wealth and trade routes of the great Indian kingdoms, the fabled riches of the East. What he found instead were the islands of the Caribbean, and what he claimed was not discovery, but possession. A possession rooted in conquest, and a conquest fueled by theological license and imperial greed.

However, Columbus was not alone. He was but one of many. While he sailed west, other European imperialists moved east and south, over land and sea, in conquest of the territories long ruled by Muslims, which they acquired through conquest, but unlike the ideologies of imperialists. Empire campaigns, dressed in the language of holy war and righteous exploration, were not merely about faith—but about resources, about land, about gold, spice, trade routes, and ultimately, about control.

And behind them stood the Roman Catholic Church, issuing spiritual cover in the form of *papal bulls—legal and theological documents that would birth the Doctrine of Discovery.* These edicts gave so-called divine authorization to European Christian powers to conquer any land not ruled by Christians. To convert. To enslave. Or to kill the brutes!

And what these colonizers were permitted to do by these edicts of the Roman Catholic Church was a brutality the world had never known— an institutionalized and theological model of conquest that made it not only acceptable but righteous to degrade, dehumanize, and destroy entire peoples.

It was a ruthless, treacherous brutality, unparalleled in scope and sanctified in holy language. It gave rise to a practice that had not been imagined in prior civilizations—to codify racial inferiority, to strip

people of their land, culture, name, god, and body, all in the name of so-called civilization.

And so when Columbus stumbled upon Haiti, he wasn't discovering—it was a collision. And what followed was not mission, but massacre. Under the banners of kingdom and cross, Columbus and his men forced the Taino people into slavery, demanded tribute, cut off hands, raped women, and murdered those who resisted.

Through the papal bulls and the Doctrine of Discovery, this violence was sacramentalized. A theology of annihilation. A gospel of empire. And so, Raoul Peck draws the line—clear, direct, unbroken:

- From the papal bulls to the plantation.
- From Columbus to Hitler.
- From the conquest of Haiti to the Shoah Memorial in Berlin.

- What the gas chambers accomplished with science, Columbus initiated with Scripture.
- What the Nazis did to Jews, Columbus had already done to the Taino people.
- What the Reich called "racial hygiene," the Church had called "civilization."

And if the world can weep at Auschwitz, but remain indifferent to the Congo, to Haiti, to Standing Rock, then Raoul asks: What do we really believe about human worth?

Because the construct of whiteness—the lie that there is a hierarchy of races, ordained by nature or God—is not an invention of the 20th century. It was seeded in 1492 by Columbus and others. Watered with gold. Fertilized with blood. Harvested in chains.

That's why the numbers matter. That's why the names matter. Because when history becomes selective, genocide becomes negotiable. And when genocide is negotiable, no one is safe!

South America Under Siege

Now the scene turns our eyes toward the continent of South America. Raoul gives attention to the continent as he states that within a hundred years, 90% of South America's way of life was under siege and detrimentally reshaped by colonizers.

This statement opens the door to one of the most devastating realities of the so-called "New World." In less than a century after first contact, entire civilizations that had thrived for thousands of years were violently upended. The Spanish and Portuguese conquests did not only seize land; they dismantled cultural, social, and spiritual frameworks, replacing them with systems of exploitation.

The Inca Empire, with its intricate network of roads and communal agricultural systems, was fractured by the Spanish conquest. Indigenous communities across the Amazon and the pampas were drawn into forced labor systems like the encomienda, which placed Native populations under the control of European settlers who extracted tribute and labor in exchange for "protection" and so-called Christian instruction. Diseases brought by Europeans—smallpox, measles, influenza—ravaged entire nations, killing millions who had no immunity.

Portuguese colonization in Brazil went further, setting the stage for the mass importation of enslaved Africans to sustain sugar plantations, creating a brutal racial caste system whose legacy lingers to this day. Jesuit missions imposed Christianity and European cultural norms, systematically erasing Indigenous traditions and languages in the name of "civilization."

When Raoul states that within a century, 90% of South America's way of life was under siege, the weight of that number becomes tangible in the historical record: cultures dismantled, millions dead, and the foundation of a continent reshaped under foreign domination.

And it wasn't without witnesses!

De las Casas' Dilemma

Enter Bartolomé de las Casas, a 16th-century Spanish Dominican friar, missionary, and historian—one of the very few Europeans who dared to write the truth. De las Casas was an eyewitness to the horrors inflicted on Indigenous Americans by the Spanish colonizers.

He saw the brutality—the burning, the mutilations, the enslavement, the mass killings—and he wrote about it with anguish. His writings, especially in his seminal work "A Short Account of the Destruction of the Indies," chronicle the atrocities committed by his fellow Spaniards: children torn from their mothers, villages obliterated, entire cultures erased.

De las Casas didn't just describe what he saw. *He was tormented by it!*

Here was his dilemma: How could Christians commit such acts—and call it God's work? How could people professing the love of Christ build empires on the bones and backs of the innocent? He wrestled not only with the violence but also with the spiritual hypocrisy. And though he began as a participant in the conquest, he eventually renounced it, dedicating his life to defending the humanity and rights of Indigenous peoples.

But even his protest was not without contradiction. In an early phase of his advocacy, de las Casas—seeking to protect Indigenous Americans—proposed using enslaved Africans instead, falsely believing they were more "fit" for the labor. Though he would later recant and regret this position, the damage of that rationale was already spreading.

And yet, even amid these contradictions, his work became a spark. It leads us to Valladolid, Spain, where in 1550, the Spanish Crown convened one of the most extraordinary debates in colonial history. Here, the documentary introduces the dramatized account of that moment: The film "The Dispute in Valladolid (1992)," directed by Jean-Daniel Verhaeghe.

The film captures a moment of deep moral reckoning in European history. It dramatizes the theological and legal debate between Bartolomé de las Casas and Juan Ginés de Sepúlveda, a prominent philosopher and humanist who defended the right of Spain to colonize and enslave Indigenous peoples.

In this disputation, Sepúlveda argued that Indigenous Americans were inferior by nature—brutes, beasts, lacking reason—and therefore subject to natural slavery under Aristotle's logic. He claimed they were incapable of self-governance and that Spanish conquest was not only justified but necessary for their own salvation.

De las Casas countered that these were fully human beings, made in the image of God, capable of reason, faith, and culture. He argued that what Spain was doing was not evangelism—it was extermination. It was a powerful moral moment—but a powerless one in practice.

Because, despite his compelling defense, the machinery of empire did not slow. The debate at Valladolid, like so many ethical questions raised in the shadow of colonization, became a symbolic performance—not a turning point, but a historical footnote in an unstoppable march of domination.

Raoul includes this moment to remind us: Even when the truth was spoken, it was ignored. Even when conscience stirred, the gold was louder. Even when moral clarity flickered, it was smothered by greed and racial ideology.

So, when Raoul shows us South America's dismemberment, he doesn't show us an accident. He shows us an inheritance. An inheritance born in 1492, debated in Valladolid and repeated across oceans and centuries. Because the theft of South America, like the annihilation of the Indigenous people elsewhere, was never a tragedy of misunderstanding.

It was policy. It was theology turned into strategy, religion turned into justification, whiteness turned into godhood. And the world is still bleeding from it!

The debate at Valladolid came and went, and history rendered its verdict—not in favor of humanity, but in favor of empire. Though Bartolomé de las Casas spoke with the voice of a witness and the heart of a confessor, colonization won. Theology gave way to strategy, and Christian morality—when placed on the scales of gold, land, and conquest—was found wanting.

And so, the documentary shifts again. Not merely to a new scene, but to a reckoning. On the screen appears a harrowing animation—a living map, stretching from the year 1501 to 1875, charting the paths of destruction carved into the world by European empires.

Dotted lines snake from the shores of West and Central Africa—arteries of stolen life—spanning the Atlantic Ocean to the Caribbean, South America, North America, Mexico, and Canada. Each line represents a slave ship. Each point, a port of misery. And what we see is not a trickle—it is a torrent. An unrelenting flood of Black bodies!

Over 12.5 million kidnapped Africans. Torn from their families. Ripped from their languages. Sold into systems designed not only to exploit their labor but to erase their humanity. And that number? That staggering, grotesque statistic? It does not include the millions who never made it.

It says nothing of those who perished—in chains, in filth, in the dark bellies of ships—during what became known as the Middle Passage. That ocean became their graveyard, and history gave them no tombstone.

But Raoul Peck will not let them be forgotten. He lifts the curtain on the lies of civilization and forces us to confront the cost of Europe's ascent: millions of shattered lives laid as the foundation for Western wealth.

And now, in the wake of these horrors, Raoul takes us into what should have been a corrective era—an age of reason, awakening, and progress. But instead, we are led into something even more insidious. We are brought face-to-face with the "Enlightenment."

CHAPTER 5

The Greatest Unmarked Cemetery in World History

This so-called "Age of Reason," spanning the 17th to 19th centuries, was the dawn of modernity—an era that birthed revolutions, rights declarations, and democratic ideals. But for the colonized world, the Enlightenment did not bring liberty. It brought new justifications for enslavement.

The Enlightenment did not dismantle white supremacy—it refined it!

Thinkers like Immanuel Kant, David Hume, Voltaire, and Thomas Jefferson spoke of freedom and reason while simultaneously promoting ideas of racial hierarchy. They claimed Africans were biologically inferior. That Indigenous peoples were undeveloped. That European civilization and the white man in particularly was the measure by which all other life should be judged.

So while European elites praised science and rationality, they wielded it as a weapon—a cloak under which slavery and genocide could march forward unchallenged. Racial categorization, phrenology, and so-called "scientific racism" became embedded into the laws, languages, and logics of empire. The very hands that held the quill of liberty also helped draw the borders of colonial control.

This is why Peck is intentional in showing us how the Enlightenment—despite its lofty ideals—enabled colonization rather than stopping it. It made exploitation look intellectual, and domination look natural. And then the documentary takes us deeper, from the philosophical to the personal, from ideology to intimacy. It leads us into the bowels of the slave ship.

The scene shifts to a powerful animation. A visceral, graphic rendering that takes us where cameras could never go—beneath the deck of a slaver's vessel. We see them: stacked like cargo, shoulder to shoulder, stripped bare of dignity and light. Black bodies pressed into darkness—shoulder to shoulder, breath upon breath, rot upon rot. No space to move. No privacy to relieve oneself. No silence to grieve. No rights. No names.

They are shown not as individuals, but as units—chattel—dehumanized in architecture specifically designed to break the soul. The animation captures what words can barely contain: The despair! The moans! The prayers. The final breaths of the forgotten.

Then, one of the enslaved Africans is shown above deck in the darkness of night. He looks out at the endless sea, while a slaver watches him—not with suspicion or fear, but with casual indifference, puffing on a cigarette like it's just another evening cruise.

And then—he leaps! The enslaved man hurls himself into the ocean's depths—not to escape, but to return. To return to a place that was never his home, but no longer his hell. To make the final choice that empire could not take from him: death over bondage. And as he sinks, the animation shifts. We are taken to the ocean floor.

There, beneath the currents, beneath the myths, beneath the whitewashed stories of triumph, we see them: countless skeletal remains, stretching endlessly across the seabed. Each one a name unknown. Each one a life stolen. The Atlantic Ocean is not just a body of water. It is a mass grave! The greatest unmarked cemetery in world history!

A watery tomb for millions whose only crime was being born into Blackness during Europe's rise to global dominance. And yet—above those same waters—monuments still rise to Columbus. Statues still honor slaveholders. Textbooks still whisper that this was "progress."

But Raoul Peck does not whisper. He shouts through silence. He calls us not only to remember, but to reckon. Because the Enlightenment promised humanity—but delivered hierarchy. And the Middle Passage did not just carry bodies. It carried the lie that some humans were not human at all.

This is not merely a story. It is a system. And it did not end in the 19th century. It merely changed its form!

As we move forward in the documentary, we find Raoul reflecting in a different register. This is no longer just historical narration; it's a lament. A meditation. A plea for understanding in the face of overwhelming horror.

His thoughts drift toward what he calls state-sponsored genocide—the deliberate, cold-blooded destruction of human life not just by rogue actors or chaotic regimes, but by governments, by nations, by so-called civilized powers. He wrestles with the core of human depravity. His voice trembles—not audibly, but through the sheer weight of his silence—as he asks a question that should shake every soul awake:

How does one human being look upon another and choose to enslave them? How can so much brutality be inflicted on a people because of the color of their skin? No doubt many are his questions, as are mine… What sort of mental, moral, and spiritual collapse must take place for such a thought to not only enter the human mind but to be normalized? To be systematized? How does such treachery become a career? A calling? A profession?

These are not intellectual questions. It is a soul-deep grief. Because the answer, though complex in history, is simple in motive: greed. Lust for wealth, land, and domination. The colonizers' hunger for power dulled their senses, deadened their consciences, and disfigured their humanity.

They no longer saw people. They saw cargo. They saw commodities. They saw numbers on ledgers and muscle in chains. They baptized their greed in religion. They cloaked it in enlightenment. And called it progress.

Enslaved White Children

Then comes the next scene. A sudden shift. The screen reads: Congo River, 1892.

At first glance, it appears to be just another reenactment. A quiet riverside, a journey upriver. We see a Black pastor, calmly seated and reading his Bible. He is dressed in colonial missionary attire, his posture composed, his faith presumably intact. By his side stands the "white man" as a guide, prepared to lead him deeper into the jungle.

But Raoul is not giving us another episode of history as told. He is flipping the script–an inversion of history. As the pastor and his guide venture inland, they hear something. The camera tightens. The music darkens. The trees part. And what they see is shocking: Dozens of white children, yes, white children—shackled, chained, herded like beasts through the forest.

Their terror is unmistakable. Their confusion visible. Their silence screaming. Driving them forward are African captors—stoic, unbothered, armed with weapons and vicious dogs. This is not history as it happened. This is history inverted. And it is meant to make you (whites) uncomfortable.

The Black clergyman is horrified. He steps forward. He pleads. He protests. He invokes moral language. But when he calls out and attempts to stop the injustice, he is forcibly stopped. His white guide calls out to silence him and stop the confrontation he had with the Black slave catcher. With a casual signal, the caravan of captive white children is ordered forward. The protest is overruled. The logic of profit once again triumphs over the logic of conscience.

What Raoul is doing here is no accident. It is a cinematic device. A provocative tool. A purposeful artistic inversion designed to unsettle and awaken! Because far too many Western white viewers can watch documentary after documentary, historical film after historical film, depicting the suffering of Africans, Indigenous peoples, and the colonized, without flinching. Without grief. Without rage.

But when the image is reversed—when white children are in chains, white skin under the yoke, white innocence led off to be sold—suddenly the conscience is jolted awake. This is not exploitation. This is exposure!

Raoul is asking the viewer:

Why must suffering look like you in order to move you?
Why must injustice reflect your face before it touches your heart?

In this imagined scene, the white children are not just victims. They are mirrors. They are there to reflect what was done to Black and brown children every day for centuries—not in fiction, but in reality, not as metaphor, but as fact. This artistic reversal is Raoul Peck's spiritual scalpel—cutting through centuries of emotional numbness, dismantling the insulation that white privilege provides.

Because what happened in the Congo was not imagined. It was real! It was brutal! It was sanctioned by kings, applauded by investors, and written out of textbooks.

This scene does not reverse history. It reveals its moral core by forcing viewers to see the brutality of colonialism not as abstract cruelty, but as intolerable, inhuman, and unjustifiable, no matter the skin color of its victims. And by doing so, Raoul helps his audience, especially white audiences, begin to grasp the truth:

That what happened to Black and Indigenous peoples under colonialism was not unfortunate. It was not accidental. It was intentional. And it was evil! Evil that could be seen more clearly—if only the faces were white.

Raoul's inversion doesn't seek to blame—it seeks to break the viewer's numbness. Because if that numbness remains, the legacy of empire will continue not just as history, but as present reality. And so this scene, though fictional in form, is truer in spirit than any reenactment. Because it dares to ask not just what happened, but why we still live with its effects and yet refuse to feel its weight. Raoul knows exactly what he's doing.

Just as the moral sensors of many white viewers begin to settle from the visual shock of enslaved white children marched through the forest, Peck gently eases the tension. He shifts the screen to something familiar, something that evokes admiration and nostalgia in the minds of many raised on the sanitized myths of empire: "The Life of Christopher Columbus," George Borgeois, 1916.

A grainy, greyish-toned portrayal of Columbus appears. A noble voyager. A man of God and the sea. We hear from Columbus's own travel journal, noting that on Thursday, October 11, 1492, he sees land. And for a brief moment, the narrative returns to a form white audiences recognize—a kind of historical lullaby. A settling back into the comfort of origin myths.

But this ease is short-lived. Raoul is not finished. Not by a long shot. Because he is not simply revisiting history—*he is dissecting mythology*. He is showing us what lies beneath the stories we were all fed, especially white viewers who have inherited history through a lens scrubbed of blood and sanitized of sin.

And so he returns again to the narrative inversion. The black pastor, once more on screen—kneeling in sincere prayer. His posture is reverent. His voice fervent. His belief in God seemingly intact. He is doing what any faithful Christian might do in the quiet morning hours: seeking divine clarity, pleading for strength.

His words are earnest. His motives appear pure. But Raoul is preparing to rupture that appearance, too. From a short distance, a new sound pierces the air. A sharp grunt. A violent rhythm. A scream swallowed in submission.

The pastor stops praying. The sounds are unmistakable. A whip. A cry. A human being in pain! And now, the pastor slowly rises and walks toward the source of the sound—unsure of what he will find, but unable to ignore what he has heard.

And then we see it: A white enslaved child, chained and tied to a tree. His back scarred, his face streaked with tears, his body quivering in anguish. Hovering above him, a Black enslaver, wielding the whip with calculated cruelty. Lashing again and again with mechanical indifference.

The camera pans—other white children, also in chains, stare wide-eyed in terror. Some look away. Others look on in silence, knowing the whip may turn on them next. There are other Black enslavers, seated nearby. Laughing. Lounging. Unmoved by the cries.

They are at ease with this violence because it is not new. Because it is normalized. Because it is profitable. The enslaved white children are merely a shipment and a commodity. The pastor draws near. His face is drawn tight with disbelief, with sorrow, with something too deep for words. And then, in a moment that rips through the soul of every viewer, he does the unthinkable.

He kicks the white child! He offers no aid. No rebuke to the enslaver. No prayer. No mercy. Instead, he becomes part of the system. He participates in the very inhumanity he was presumed to oppose.

And Raoul is not showing us this to invert history for the sake of provocation. He is not interested in shock without purpose. He is performing a moral transplant. Because this is what Africans lived through—day after day, century after century.

They were not just whipped! They were not just sold! They were betrayed by those who claimed piety. Beaten by men who carried Bibles. Kicked by so-called Christians who knelt in prayer one hour and sanctioned bloodshed the next.

Raoul wants white audiences to feel what it means to watch someone who looks like them stripped of humanity, mercy, and protection. And more than that, he is forcing viewers to ask: Why does this disturb me more than when it was Black children? Why is my moral imagination more activated when the victim looks like me?

It is a test. A confrontation. A cinematic sermon.

The Black pastor in this inversion is not a historical figure—he is a mirror. A reflection of every priest, missionary, or silent bystander who claimed the name of Christ while standing in the shadow of a whip.

Because the pastor's prayer was not enough. Because faith without justice is complicity.

Raoul's brilliance is that he does not need to fabricate new horrors. He only needs to reverse the lens. In doing so, he exposes the grotesque symmetry of colonial violence—how it operated, how it was rationalized, and how it continues to be minimized in the telling of history. This scene is a cinematic reckoning. A moral rebuke. A radical act of empathy through inversion.

Because the truth is, millions of African children were whipped just like that. And no pastor stopped it. No teacher taught against it. No empire apologized for it.

So, Raoul Peck takes us there—not to rewrite history, but to make us finally feel it! Because until the privileged conscience is pierced, the systems of supremacy will remain intact!

The Weaponization of Words

The scene shifts again. We see the word: Nègre. Then another: Negro.

And with them, the story of language as a weapon begins to unfold. Raoul doesn't need to explain it directly—because the words themselves do the talking. Nègre—a French distortion, once merely descriptive, now twisted to mean something subhuman. Negro—a racial epithet codified into every system of law, commerce, and violence from Europe to the Americas.

These words did not merely describe—they defined. They were used to categorize, to debase, to strip away personhood and to create an enduring psychological scaffold for oppression. Raoul reveals how language was not just a mirror of racism, but its tool and accomplice. Because when you name someone a "nègre" or a "negro," you are not naming them as a human.

You are marking them! Branding them!

You are creating a chasm that no faith, no logic, no justice can cross—unless the name itself is dismantled. It was this perversion of language—infused with contempt and carried on the tongues of "civilized" men—that helped fuel the spread of the transatlantic slave trade, the theological justifications of conquest, and the so-called scientific racism that would soon take root.

For as slavery expanded and empires stretched across the globe, a more insidious support system emerged—one masked as intellectual inquiry and Enlightenment progress: pseudoscience. This was no longer just a cultural bias—it was now being written into the textbooks, preached from universities, published in journals, and taught as truth.

Phrenology—the measuring of skulls—declared that Africans had smaller cranial capacity and thus were intellectually inferior.

Physiognomy—the reading of facial features–was used to claim moral degeneracy based on skin tone.

Polygenism—the theory that different races originated from different biological origins—argued that Black people were not even part of the same human family as whites.

Figures such as Carl Linnaeus, the Swedish naturalist, classified humans into racial hierarchies with the African at the bottom—lazy, lustful, governed by impulse. Later thinkers like Josiah Nott, Samuel Morton, and Louis Agassiz used distorted data to "prove" that whiteness was the evolutionary pinnacle of humanity. This was not science; it was indoctrination by another name. A system of fabricated evidence designed to justify colonization, slavery, and extermination.

By the mid-18th and 19th centuries, these falsehoods were being used to legitimize European domination as natural, even noble. Colonizers claimed they were not only expanding territory—they were elevating the lesser races, bringing light to darkness, taming the savage. Thus, scientific racism became the intellectual backbone of white supremacy.

It was used to shape policies, build museums, construct immigration laws, control reproduction through eugenics, and even define national identity.

This wasn't fringe theory—it was mainstream ideology across Europe and the Americas. And it laid the groundwork for centuries of violence. Because once a people are declared biologically inferior, their enslavement is no longer a moral question—*it becomes a scientific inevitability.*

This is why Raoul begins with words. Because words—"Nègre," "Negro," "beast," "brute," "savage"—pave the way for ideologies. And ideologies pave the way for systems. And systems produce the tools to enslave, to exterminate, and to silence.

The Haitian Revolution

And then the scene shifts again. "The Age of Revolutions."

An era long celebrated in Western textbooks. The American Revolution in 1776—"liberty or death." The French Revolution in 1789—"liberté, égalité, fraternité." The Industrial Revolution and the Enlightenment—all hailed as signs of human progress, reason, and liberation. But what is almost always forgotten—or intentionally omitted—is that in this same period, a revolution occurred that shattered the logic of racial hierarchy and white supremacy.

The Haitian Revolution. The year is 1791.

In the French colony of Saint-Domingue, one of the most brutal slave regimes on earth, enslaved Africans rise up—not just to protest, but to overthrow an empire. This revolution wasn't sparked by theory. It was sparked by the lash, by the chains, by the unyielding conviction that Black people were human beings with the right to be free.

This was not a footnote in history; it was an earthquake!

Raoul does not miss the opportunity to highlight what white textbooks diminish. Because the Haitian Revolution, led by men like Toussaint Louverture, Jean-Jacques Dessalines, Henri Christophe, and later shaped by the political navigation of Alexandre Pétion, was the first successful slave revolt in the history of the world.

It was not given. It was fought for, bled for, died for. The result? The first Black republic in the so-called New World. An independent nation born not of European benevolence but of African resistance. It was a revolution that terrified every enslaver from Virginia to Havana to London.

Because what Haiti represented was a radical contradiction to the very idea of white supremacy. Haiti said: ***Your race is not divine. Your power is not ordained. Your empire can fall—and we will be the ones to topple it!***

And it did not just inspire fear, it inspired hope. From the shores of Brazil to the plantations of the Carolinas, word spread of what had happened in Saint-Domingue. The enslaved now knew that revolt was possible. That the world could be changed by those whom it tried to crush.

But instead of acknowledging this revolution as one of the greatest in human history, white powers responded with silence—and economic vengeance. Haiti would be made to suffer!

Its economy isolated. Its sovereignty undermined. And its success in freedom punished by those who once claimed to love liberty. Because the Haitian Revolution exposed the lie at the heart of Western civilization: That liberty was for all.

Raoul knows that this omission is no accident. It is deliberate. Because to celebrate Haiti would require the West to confront its hypocrisy. To honor Louverture would mean dethroning Washington. To teach Dessalines would mean challenging Jefferson.

And so, they are erased!

But in Exterminate All the Brutes, their names are lifted. Their sacrifices remembered. Their revolution reinserted into the center of the story. Because the truth is, while Europe dressed itself in Enlightenment rhetoric, it was still sharpening its knives. While France spoke of fraternity, it refused to release its slaves. While America cried liberty, it expanded its slave plantations.

It was Haiti, not the West, that first actualized the true meaning of revolution for the enslaved and the colonized. And that is why they buried it. But Raoul unburies it.

He puts the Haitian Revolution not in the margins, but at the heart. Because it is not just a chapter of history, it is a rebuttal to everything empire claimed to be.

The Haitian Revolution did more than defy the racial logic of white supremacy. It shook the economic engine of slavery in the Western Hemisphere. Its tremors were not contained to the island of Hispaniola. They rippled outward—across oceans, across empires, across centuries. The machine—that monstrous, grinding system of slavery—began to sputter under the weight of what Haiti accomplished.

Because in Haiti, Blackness fought back. And the effects were immediate. By 1811, Puerto Rico began to feel the pressure. In 1816, the United

Provinces of South America broke free. Chile, 1818. Gran Colombia, 1819. Peru, 1821. Mexico, 1821. And the list grows.

Not all abolished slavery immediately, but Haiti planted the seed. Because the mere existence of a successful Black republic sent fear through the veins of every colonial government. What had seemed unthinkable—the reversal of power, the collapse of white control—was now undeniably real.

The Haitian Revolution became proof that the grip of slavery was not eternal. That those shackled and dehumanized could bring empire to its knees. Western imperialists could not fathom it. This event, born from the depths of their cruelty, had outmaneuvered their expectations, outlasted their might, and overturned their world!

It was an earthquake in history—a defiance so total, it not only challenged their economic systems, but exposed the cracks in their science, their theology, and their imagined racial hierarchies. But instead of standing back, instead of leaving well enough alone, the machine attempted to restart.

And at its helm stood Napoleon Bonaparte—arrogant, imperial, unrelenting. Unable to accept defeat, Napoleon sent an army of 65,000 troops to the island, intent on re-enslaving a people who had already tasted freedom. It was not just a military campaign. It was a campaign against Black sovereignty, against the right of African-descended people to govern themselves, against the very idea that they could stand equal to the white world.

But Napoleon miscalculated. Greatly! His forces were decimated—not only by fierce Haitian resistance, but by the land itself. By its heat. Its disease. And the resolve of a people who would never go back to the whip! *The cost was staggering! And the consequence was monumental!*

Napoleon, now weakened and desperate for cash, turned to another imperial project: the Louisiana Territory. And in 1803, France sold it to the United States. This was the so-called Louisiana Purchase—a massive land acquisition that doubled the size of the young American republic. While displacing tens of thousands of Native Americans and killing thousands!

But let history be clear: *The Louisiana Purchase was only made possible because Haiti defeated Napoleon.* Because Black men and women broke the French war machine, forcing Napoleon to abandon his dreams of a Western empire. So the irony is bitter and profound.

The freedom won by Haitians was used to expand the land of their oppressors. The bloodshed in Haiti fertilized the soil of American expansion and future enslavement. And that expansion would come with a double cost.

Because of the unimaginable success of the Haitian revolt, America was able to push westward with newfound urgency and justification—claiming lands across the Mississippi and beyond. But this expansion not only meant the growth of the slave economy, it also required the systematic removal, displacement, and destruction of Native American peoples.

As new territories were opened, there was now more land to be worked, more cotton to be harvested, more profit to be made. And so the demand for enslaved African labor intensified, tethering Black suffering to the soil of westward conquest. But to plant that cotton and build that wealth, Indigenous Americans had to be removed.

What followed was a long and brutal campaign of betrayal, broken treaties, and bloodshed. Land was seized. Tribes were scattered. Lives were lost. The very soil purchased through Black resistance became the stage for both Black enslavement and Native erasure!

The torch of oppression simply changed hands—burning through both African and Indigenous lives alike. Raoul's lens doesn't let us forget that. The cost of empire is never paid by the empire. It is paid in stolen breath, in broken backs, in vanished names and silenced songs.

So when Haiti shattered the French empire, America picked up the pieces—and built a new one of its own.

Caged and Commodified

While Peck, through his masterful lens, has thus far exposed many layers of empire, violence, and historical amnesia, I now step into this moment to shine a piercing and unapologetic light on one of the most grotesque manifestations of white supremacy: the spectacle of racial dehumanization.

Let the record show that the colonizers did not stop at stealing land, stealing labor, or stealing life. They went even further—they stole dignity. They turned Blackness, Indigeneity, and all non-European existence into an object of entertainment. A curiosity! A spectacle!

Across the 19th and early 20th centuries, European and American societies institutionalized the public display of nonwhite bodies—in zoos, in circuses, in museums, and at world fairs—under the thin veneer of science, anthropology, and "civilized" curiosity. But let there be no confusion: this was barbarism dressed in white collars and lab coats.

And among the many lives desecrated by this cruelty, two names cry out from history: *Ota Benga and Sarah Baartman*. Ota Benga, a young Congolese man, was captured and purchased by an American missionary after his family was slaughtered during Belgium's imperial conquest of the Congo—a conquest we now understand to be one of the most brutal genocides of the modern era. In 1906, Ota Benga was put on display at the Bronx Zoo in New York City. Not in a guest house. Not in a lecture hall. But in a cage. With chimpanzees and orangutans.

There he stood, humiliated before crowds of gawking white families, as if he were an animal to be observed rather than a man to be respected. The zookeepers even gave him bones to chew on to complete the illusion of savagery. People came by the thousands—laughing, pointing, jeering.

A man—a human being made in the image of God—turned into a living exhibit in the world's so-called beacon of freedom and democracy. His life ended in tragedy. After years of mental torment, exclusion, and despair, Ota Benga died by suicide in 1916.

Then there was Sarah Baartman, a Khoikhoi woman from South Africa, known cruelly by Europeans as the "Hottentot Venus." In the early 1800s, she was taken to Europe and paraded on stages in London and Paris, where she was stripped, ogled, and objectified. White audiences paid to stare at her body—especially her buttocks—fetishizing her physical features as if she were a creature of myth, not a woman with breath and soul.

They mocked her. Prodded her. Measured her. Degraded her. Even after her death in 1815, the cruelty did not end. Her body was dissected, her genitalia preserved in jars, and her skeleton displayed in the Musée de l'Homme in Paris until 1974. It took until 2002—nearly two centuries—for her remains to be returned to her homeland and laid to rest with dignity. These were not isolated cases.

Throughout Europe and the Americas, human zoos flourished. In 1889, the Paris World's Fair featured an entire "Negro village," with 400 Africans displayed like livestock. In 1904, the St. Louis World's Fair exhibited over 1,000 Filipinos in "tribal villages," mocking their customs and portraying them as primitives in need of white governance. From Dahomey villages in Belgium to Aboriginal exhibits in Australia, this cruel theater of racism spanned continents. Scientific racism gave it a script. Colonial power gave it a stage. And white society gave it applause.

They labeled Africans as "missing links" between apes and humans. They measured skulls to fabricate hierarchies of intelligence. They invented phrenology, eugenics, and anthropometry to cloak their hatred in data. But make no mistake: what they called "science" was sin.

What they called "education" was indoctrination. What they called "curiosity" was cruelty. This was not civilization. It was savagery draped in a lab coat. It was empire playing God. And it was a deep, soul-rending offense to the image of God in every human being of color that ever lived, or died, beneath the crushing gaze of white voyeurism.

To those who say history is the past, we say: Not until truth is told. Not until names are restored. Not until justice breathes.

We remember Ota Benga. We honor Sarah Baartman.

And we speak for the unnamed, the dismembered, the caged, and the commodified. Because history, if it does not weep, is not history at all!

Who are We?

Just when the viewer believes that the documentary has exhausted its capacity for critique—its sharp indictments of empire, its painful recoveries of hidden histories—Raoul Peck turns inward. The camera pans through different moments of Raoul's story told through film. The lens captures Raoul's memories of his past. And we are reminded that history is not only vast. It is also intimate. It lives not just in footnotes, maps, or museums, but in memory, family, and heartbreak.

The documentary now shifts from the deconstruction of empires to the reconstruction of the self. The screen pans over the cityscape of Rome. Raoul says, "This is where I fell in love." And it becomes clear: this history is not academic. This is personal. Painfully, beautifully, undeniably personal.

Raoul opens his heart. He makes mention of his mother, a woman no doubt of strength, resilience, and grace. He then introduces us to his father—a man of certainty, of vision and conviction, no doubt shaped by the turbulence of Haiti's past and its uncertain future. He tells us of his own child, who was born in Uganda and attended school in New Jersey. The birth of new life—his daughter, yet raised in a world still steeped in old lies.

And then he speaks of one of his three brothers, a brother who served in the military, only to return broken by what that service cost him. PTSD became his private war—a war that so many veterans, especially Black and brown soldiers, are left to fight alone after the medals are pinned and the flags are folded.

His two additional accomplished brothers are also mentioned. And with each name, Raoul does not just tell a story; he constructs an identity. Piece by piece. Memory by memory. He is not just building a biography. He is asking a question. "Who am I?"

And then again—more layered, more collective, more urgent: *"Who are we?"*

It is the question that haunts every person shaped by the violence of empire, by the dislocation of migration, by the fracture of identity under white domination. Raoul confesses: "I have traveled to many places… but they were never called my own." This is not just about geography; it's about alienation. About being in a world that was never meant to hold your dignity, your truth, your belonging. He shares memories of being a child—moving, playing, learning. Then memories as an adult—working and loving. And yet the question lingers in every room, every land, every language.

"These places were not my home." He tells us, almost with both pride and ache, "I have built homes in Cuba." But even then, in the warmth of love or the walls constructed by his own hands, he returns again to the refrain: "Who am I?"

This is not indecision—it's resistance. It's a refusal to let others name him. A rejection of the forced identities colonizers have tried to brand onto the backs of the displaced. To ask "Who am I?" again and again is to say, I will not settle for your answer. I will find my own.

And it is into this emotional moment that Raoul introduces a name that, for Haitians and students of Caribbean politics, looms large: The name appears starkly on the screen: Jean-Bertrand Aristide – 1991. A priest. A populist. A man who rose to become President of Haiti with the promise of dignity, justice, and revolution in his mouth.

Raoul speaks of Aristide not just as a political figure, but as a symbol of hope—a man who once stirred in him the belief that maybe, just maybe, Haiti could become what it had always deserved to be: free, sovereign, and whole. But that hope, like so many before it, unraveled.

Peck does not go into exhaustive political detail, but his tone says enough. There was disappointment. There was disillusionment. The very man who once stood against foreign exploitation would later be perceived by many as complicit in the same systems he opposed.

Whether through external pressures, internal compromises, or the crushing weight of imperial sabotage, Aristide's presidency became a complicated symbol of the postcolonial tragedy: how leaders born of resistance are often consumed by the very systems they once fought to dismantle.

Peck's pain is palpable. He loved Haiti enough to believe in Aristide. And that belief—like the dreams of so many children of diaspora—was betrayed. This moment is not a detour from the documentary's themes. It is the heart of them. Because what is colonization, if not the theft of hope? What is white supremacy, if not the breaking of faith in self, in family, in nation?

Raoul's question, "Who am I?"—does not end in despair. It lingers. It challenges.

Because to ask, "Who am I?" is to reject every false identity imposed by empire. It is to claim one's own name—with all its contradictions, complexities, and truths. And so, we sit with Raoul—not just as viewers of history, but as participants in it. We feel the ache of loving a country that has known too much betrayal. We wrestle with the tension between dream and reality, between freedom and its fragile pursuit. And we remember: the greatest revolutions are not only fought on battlefields. They are fought in the soul.

The Scots-Irish's Violent Ethos: The Confederacy and Birth of the KKK

As the documentary continues, the screen displays a grotesque phrase—"The Irish Apes." A name not born of satire, but of white supremacist pseudoscience and imperial propaganda. It is here that Raoul Peck takes us back to the British Empire's ruthless conquest of Ireland.

The Irish were not merely occupied—they were dehumanized. In the minds of English colonizers, they were not fellow Christians, not even fellow Europeans. No, the Irish were imagined as less than human—descendants of apes, in contrast to the "refined" English who considered themselves direct descendants of Adam. This brutal racial mythology was the prototype for colonial racism.

The conquest of Ireland, especially during the Tudor and Stuart periods, was a horror show of massacres, land seizures, and forced anglicization. Catholic practices were banned. The Irish language was criminalized. Families were separated. Culture was targeted for annihilation.

And from this crucible of trauma emerged a sub-group—the Scots-Irish—descendants of Lowland Scots and English settlers who were planted in Northern Ireland to act as colonial proxies. They were used by the British Crown to enforce imperial control, and in return, they were given land

and status. But even they were hardened by conflict. And it would not be long before they exported this colonial violence to the Americas.

With land lost and hardship severe, many Scots-Irish—like their Native Irish neighbors—emigrated to North America. But while many Irish immigrants arrived poor and disenfranchised, the Scots-Irish often brought with them the tactics and mindset of empire. They had been enforcers of colonization in Ulster, and they quickly became its agents in the so-called New World.

On screen appears another chilling title, "Methods of Genocide."

Listed:

- Slavery… Deportation
- Sterilization… Mutilation
- Massacre… Destruction of Cultural Symbols
- Starvation… Forceful Conversions
- Separation of families

These methods were first refined against the Irish and then unleashed with renewed force in North America. The Scots-Irish carried with them a violent ethos. They saw the frontier not as a place of coexistence, but as a battlefield. And so they turned their weapons, first honed in the hills of Ireland, against Native American tribes and enslaved Africans.

They settled disproportionately in the Appalachian regions and along the violent edge of the American frontier. And there, they waged a bloody campaign against Indigenous peoples. Tribes such as the Cherokee, Shawnee, Creek, and others bore the brunt of their expansionist drive.

Scots-Irish settlers did not merely occupy the land—they saw themselves as fulfilling a divine destiny.

They began to identify as a "Chosen People," heirs to the biblical covenant, commissioned by God to conquer a "wilderness" and build a new Israel. This was not religion in the service of truth. It was religion weaponized—a theology of domination. The land was theirs because they wrongly believed God had ordained it, and any people who stood in their way—Native Americans, enslaved Africans, even other whites—were seen as Canaanites to be driven out or destroyed.

Their Calvinist theology was often laced with millenarianism, and it fused seamlessly with white supremacy. This theological framework became one of the ideological engines for settler colonialism, Manifest Destiny, and ultimately, Southern secessionism.

The Scots-Irish played a disproportionately large role in the Confederate Army. Many of its generals, including Stonewall Jackson, J.E.B. Stuart, and Nathan Bedford Forrest, hailed from Scots-Irish lineages. Forrest, of course, would go on to become the first Grand Wizard of the Ku Klux Klan and the terror he inspired was built on a tradition of white dominance that the Scots-Irish had been conditioned to accept as righteous.

But even before the Civil War, the Scots-Irish were enforcers of slavery. They served in slave patrols—paramilitary groups sanctioned by the state to track down runaways, terrorize Black communities, and uphold racial order. These patrols were not isolated acts of cruelty; they were the precursors to modern policing in the American South.

And the violence was not limited to the physical. The Scots-Irish settlers contributed to the ideological and cultural frameworks of white supremacy. They passed laws that codified Black inferiority. They helped build schools, churches, and governments that normalized the subjugation of non-white peoples. And when the Union won the Civil War, many Scots-Irish communities became hotbeds of resistance—fostering *Lost Cause mythology*, segregation, and anti-Black terrorism for generations to come.

The Lost Cause mythology is a revisionist myth that falsely portrays the Confederacy as a noble, moral, and heroic movement unrelated to slavery, which they downplayed as a desired and welcomed outcome for the enslaved. It is historically inaccurate and was used to uphold white supremacy and undermine racial progress after the Civil War.

In short, these colonial settlers' legacy is complex, but clear: A people forged by empire in Ireland became, in many cases, the instruments of empire in America. And as Raoul Peck continues to peel back the layers of history, he makes it impossible to deny: The methods of genocide that ravaged Africa and the Americas were not born overnight.

They were practiced. Refined. Perfected. And the Scots-Irish, with Bible in one hand and rifle in the other, became some of its fiercest practitioners.

CHAPTER 6

America: A Nation of Immigrants - A Paradox

The screen transitions in on the solemn moments of presidential oaths. On the screen appears, "In the Name of God."

First, Franklin D. Roosevelt is shown taking his oath and ending with the traditional "So help me God." Then, clips follow of at least six other presidents—each raising a hand and concluding their oath in the same manner, thereby claiming loyalty to the state. While the documentary doesn't name them explicitly, they are clearly recognizable as:

- Harry S. Truman
- Dwight D. Eisenhower
- John F. Kennedy
- Ronald Reagan
- Barack Obama
- Donald Trump

This sequence is offered to reveal more than pomp—it shows a foundational symbolism: it may be for some of these leaders that they are publicly invoking divine legitimacy before pledging loyalty—not just to the Constitution or people, but to a divine mandate.

Where this is the case, it's a troubling pattern:

- They claim God's backing.
- They present themselves as the "elect of God."

Therefore, like the colonizers before them, being under divine mandate, they had a right to deal with the "Indigenous Peoples" as they deemed necessary. Furthermore, they defined "election" by wealth and skin color, assuming that prosperity is a sign of divine favor, while poverty and dark skin indicate moral or even spiritual deficiency and damnation.

Through this lens, colonizers cast themselves as predestined for virtue, echoing Puritan ideology. These were the beliefs of the Massachusetts Pilgrims, 41 of whom invoked God's name as they seized and claimed Indigenous lands.

America is often called "a nation of immigrants." But Raoul points to the glaring paradox: A country built on diversity—Yet defined by violence. Why? Because whiteness and power demanded control. Because self-proclaimed chosenness justified conquest. Because when leaders cry "God bless America," they also bless:

- Slavery
- Genocide
- Exclusion

Raoul's observation is neither cynical nor contrarian—it is rooted in historical fact: America's origin as a diverse nation didn't inoculate it against brutality. Rather, that diversity often became the pretext for even deeper hierarchy, policing, and violence. Its openness coexisted with its opportunistic conquest. So what does Raoul want us to take away?

He is pointing out a foundational tension in America's story: If you believe America is a nation of immigrants and a beacon of liberty, then you must also confront the history where liberty was denied to millions—Native Americans, enslaved Africans, migrants without whiteness. Raoul is calling upon us not to choose between pride or guilt—but to face both with honesty.

The documentary now presses into one of the most searing contradictions at the heart of the American narrative—the myth that the United States is a nation of immigrants, a land of welcome, a refuge for the tired, the poor, the huddled masses yearning to breathe free. Raoul Peck refuses to let this go unchallenged. For what does this promise mean to those who are not of European descent?

The scene shifts as Raoul directs our attention to the lived experience of non-European immigrants, Indigenous Americans, Mexicans (who are not immigrants), and others whose ancestry predates the very nation that now marginalizes them. These are people who work, who serve, who sacrifice, who pledge allegiance, who wave the American flag not as a threat but as a symbol of their hope, fidelity, and dignity. And yet, that fidelity is too often met with suspicion, dismissal, and contempt.

In powerful juxtaposition, the documentary illustrates how embracing "the white way"—in dress, language, mannerisms, or worldview—offers no guarantee of acceptance, no assurance of equal treatment. For non-whites, full humanity remains conditional. Whiteness is not just a skin color—it's a protected status, a measure of social acceptability and legal protection that cannot simply be adopted by assimilation. You cannot dress yourself into whiteness. You cannot salute yourself into acceptance.

Then the scene shifts again, flashing through time, showing a rapid succession of televised and widely circulated moments of racialized violence. The images speak! The faces tell their own stories. Black and brown bodies under siege. What some will call state-sanctioned brutality witnessed. Sirens… Then George Floyd appears in the footage.

His name needs no context, no timestamp. His death, captured in high definition beneath the crushing knee of a police officer, became a global cry. Raoul uses these images not as spectacle, but as reckoning—a reminder that the brutality of colonialism did not die with the age of empires. It evolved. It rebranded. It now wears badges and claims the language of law and order. But the result is the same: domination, degradation, death.

This moment in the documentary pierces deep, showing that America's invitation to "your tired, your poor" has always been selective, conditional, and often violently hypocritical. Peck is making clear that the same structures that enslaved, colonized, and dehumanized in the past are alive today—not as relics, but as policies, attitudes, and systems. A knee that crushed George Floyd is a direct descendant of the whips that lashed African backs, the bullets that massacred Native People, and the cages that confined immigrant children.

And yet Raoul does not allow us to look away. Not from the violence. Not from the contradiction. Not from the America that calls itself a land of liberty while building its foundation on domination. He leaves the viewer not just with a feeling, but with a question:

What will we do with the truth now that we can no longer claim we didn't see it?

Teachers of Truth: Howard Zinn and Roxanne Dunbar-Ortiz

The scene now shifts—ocean waves crash beneath darkened skies, a brooding sea symbolic of the storm that is both historical and present. Vast, seemingly endless, the turbulent waters mirror the generational trauma and the global wreckage wrought by colonization and white supremacy. As the winds of truth howl and the tides churn, the screen presents the names of two guiding voices: Howard Zinn and Roxanne Dunbar-Ortiz.

Raoul Peck, with profound reverence, invokes these two historians—not simply as scholars but as elders in the struggle. Teachers of truth. Guides through the fog of sanitized history. He learns from them not as one memorizing facts, but as a disciple drinking deeply from a wellspring of moral clarity.

Howard Zinn, the late people's historian, is best known for his groundbreaking work, A People's History of the United States (1980). In this work, Zinn turned historical narrative on its head, shifting the lens from conquerors, presidents, and industrialists to the enslaved, the workers, the Indigenous, the immigrants, the resistors. Zinn dared to center the oppressed, giving voice to those who had been crushed beneath the machinery of American exceptionalism. Through Zinn, Raoul inherits a framework of historical reimagination—one that interrogates empire, questions legitimacy, and exposes the price of progress when paid in blood.

Zinn wrote: "There is no flag large enough to cover the shame of killing innocent people." This sentiment pulses through Exterminate All the Brutes like a heartbeat. It is echoed in Raoul's narration, in the images of conquest, in the bones buried beneath the Atlantic.

Roxanne Dunbar-Ortiz, the living elder, furthers this excavation of truth. Her work, An Indigenous Peoples' History of the United States (2014), confronts the foundational myths of the American republic by centering the perspective of Native Peoples. She pulls the veil off *Manifest Destiny, revealing it as a theology of death.* She shows how the American project has always been about land theft, racial hierarchy, and elimination—first of Native Peoples, then of all who could not be folded into whiteness.

Dunbar-Ortiz writes: "The founding myth of the United States is white supremacy. Violence is its engine." Raoul drinks deeply from her well, weaving her conclusions into his cinematic fabric. He does not merely quote her—he shows her assertions, framing them with footage of burning villages, mutilated bodies, erased histories.

In honoring Zinn and Dunbar-Ortiz, Raoul invites his viewers—especially white viewers—not just to listen, but to unlearn. To surrender the sanitized stories passed down by textbooks and national holidays. To sit at the feet of truth-tellers and inherit a more painful, but more honest, understanding of our shared world.

And in that space of reverence, Raoul offers one of his most powerful ethical conclusions: "We are to see ourselves as one." Not above. Not superior. But a collective. A human family. This is not an idealistic plea for colorblindness. It is a moral imperative, rooted in historical consequence. Because every time one group raised itself above another, claiming chosenness, claiming purity, claiming dominion—it led to chains, to fire, to blood.

So, Raoul learns from Zinn. Learns from Dunbar-Ortiz. And like them, he teaches: We cannot undo the past, but we can stop lying about it. We can stop building monuments to murderers and myths. We can choose truth over comfort. And in doing so, we can begin to rehumanize not only those we have dehumanized but perhaps, at last, even ourselves.

"Age of Jackson"

The screen fades in with bold white text against the background of wilderness, Indigenous Native Americans' land: "The Case of Andrew Jackson." It is not just a case study in one man's life—but a case study in American hypocrisy, brutality, and the enduring lie of liberty. The documentary dissects the myth of Andrew Jackson, peeling back the gilded veneer that American textbooks have long used to cover the stench of conquest.

Raoul Peck challenges viewers to reject the sanitized tale of the "Age of Jackson," so often lauded in academic circles as the birth of democracy for the common man. But as this documentary makes unequivocally clear, Jackson's democracy was never intended for Native Americans, Africans, or women. His "common man" was white, male, Protestant—and violent. The foundations of Jacksonian democracy were built not on principles of liberty, but on a mountain of bones and a sea of blood.

Andrew Jackson was born in 1767 in the Carolinas, descended from Scots-Irish Protestant immigrants—a group already discussed for the fierce and brutal traditions they carried from the conquest of Ireland to the shores of

North America. That same zeal and ferocity for domination, land acquisition, and racial hierarchy lived in Jackson's bones.

Before his rise to national fame, Jackson had already embedded himself in the colonial machinery of land theft. As a judge in **Tennessee**, he used the weight of legal authority to seize Native American lands, often under the pretense of lawful transfer or broken treaties—treaties that he and others like him had no intention of honoring. He wielded judicial power not as a tool of justice, but as a weapon of imperialism.

But it was as a military general and later as the 7th President of the United States that Jackson revealed the full scope of his brutality. The documentary rightfully points to what must be named plainly: genocide. The forced displacement of entire tribes—most notoriously through the Indian Removal Act of 1830—was not an unfortunate consequence of progress. It was a deliberate policy of *ethnic cleansing*.

The Trail of Tears, which claimed the lives of thousands of Cherokee, Creek, Chickasaw, Choctaw, and Seminole peoples, was the result of Jackson's cold calculus of conquest. His ambition was land, and the Native peoples were merely obstacles to be pushed aside, starved out, marched to death, or erased entirely.

And while he was marching Indigenous peoples off their ancestral lands, Jackson was also building his personal empire through the ownership of enslaved Africans. The documentary notes that Jackson's first recorded purchase of an enslaved person was a 21-year-old Black woman, whom he bought in 1788. From there, his holdings grew. By the time he was president, he owned over 150 enslaved people who worked his Hermitage plantation in Tennessee. He profited from their labor, whipped their backs, and broke their spirits—all while preaching the virtues of democracy.

This contradiction—of freedom proclaimed and slavery enforced—is not an aberration in American history. It is the blueprint. And Andrew Jackson, lionized on currency and carved into the annals of patriotic lore, is one of its chief architects.

Let it be stated plainly: the genocide of Native peoples was not caused by disease or inferior technology alone. That is a comforting lie. The extermination came because colonizers, like Jackson, were willing to kill, manipulate, and deceive to take land that did not belong to them. They were driven by lust for land, greed for resources, and the arrogant certainty that they were entitled to dominion over all others. This is not democracy. This is the desecration of humanity for profit and power.

Raoul Peck forces us to look, not away. To see Jackson not through the lens of nostalgia, but through the eyes of those he displaced, enslaved, and destroyed.

Then appears, in bold red letters, the word "GENOCIDIST" followed in white by the words: Responsibility. Intent. Motivation. Feeling of Guilt. Demoralization. These words are not simply rhetorical; they are accusations. They force the viewer to confront the ideological and moral machinery that enabled the mass killing of Indigenous peoples. These weren't accidents of history. They were calculated decisions fueled by greed, racial hatred, and a belief in divine entitlement.

Jesup: The Embodiment of A Henchman

At this point, the documentary focuses on Quartermaster General Thomas Sidney Jesup, a largely forgotten figure in most textbooks, but described here as "the embodiment of every other henchman of history." Jesup's role during the Second Seminole War included treachery and cruelty, such as the notorious capture of Seminole leader Osceola under a false flag of truce—a betrayal that exemplified the American government's pattern of deception against Native nations.

The documentary now offers a haunting and cinematic juxtaposition. Thomas Sidney Jesup, the ruthless Quartermaster General, infamous for his role in the Seminole Wars, is shown bathing alone in a still, shallow riverbed, shirtless, contemplative. His presence is eerie. The river, a symbol of life, baptism, or perhaps attempted cleansing, is disrupted as Raoul Peck merges history with the present, creating a seamless bridge between colonial savagery and modern white nationalism.

As Jesup lifts his head, the camera turns his gaze outward. In the distance, a modern pickup truck appears, its bed flying a massive American flag. Trailing behind the truck are a group of white men, shouting from unseen mouths, but their chant echoes in the atmosphere: "You will not replace us!" The phrase, burned into American memory during the 2017 Charlottesville rally, is not simply a contemporary outburst—it is the echo of a colonial ideology, passed from the mouths of Jesup and Jackson to the throats of modern extremists. It is the cry of those clinging to stolen ground, still determined to defend the legacy of conquest and exclusion.

And then—just as the voices fade—a piece of paper floats gently down the river toward Jesup. He catches it, unfolds it, and reads the chilling headline: "Attempted Assassination of Andrew Jackson." This surreal and symbolic moment forces the viewer to wrestle with history's long shadow. Jesup and Jackson are not merely figures of the past. Their ideology, their policies, their violent justifications still shape America's present. Raoul's camera is not simply showing us memory. It is showing us continuity.

The screen now displays the words: Treaty of the Hickory Ground, 1814. This treaty, signed under duress at the end of the Creek War, was another legal mechanism by which Andrew Jackson extracted land from Native hands. The Creek (Muscogee) people, having lost the Battle of Horseshoe Bend, were compelled to cede over 20 million acres of ancestral territory to the United States—a staggering theft that paved the way for the future states of Alabama and Georgia.

Jackson's hunger for land was insatiable. But it wasn't just about territory; it was about what the land could generate: cotton, labor, capital, and power. The colonizer mindset did not view Indigenous peoples as sovereign nations but as impediments to empire. In this spirit, Andrew Jackson made his infamous declaration that it was "absurd to make treaties with Indians," because to do so would imply that they were "a nation of sovereign people"—an idea fundamentally rejected by settler colonial ideology. The doctrine of conquest could not coexist with recognition of Indigenous humanity.

And then enters another voice—John Caldwell Calhoun, a staunch defender of slavery and states' rights, who declared unapologetically that *"slavery is a necessary evil."* This remark wasn't just a reflection of Southern arrogance. It was the intellectual backbone of white supremacy and an admission that American prosperity depended on the subjugation and dehumanization of others. Calhoun and Jackson, though different in approach, were united in purpose: to expand white dominion, regardless of the cost to Indigenous, Black, or non-white lives.

Raoul Peck stitches these voices together across time, revealing that their legacy is not confined to history books, but is breathed into modern America. The ideology of Jackson and Calhoun animates present policy, fuels contemporary violence, and echoes in chants from the mouths of neo-nationalists who fly the same flag that once flew over Indian removal and slavery.

In highlighting Jesup bathing as white nationalists chant in the background, and placing Jackson and Calhoun's words in full historical and moral view, the documentary exposes the through-line between genocide, greed, and modern extremism. Jesup, Jackson, Calhoun—they are not relics. They are reflections, and Raoul Peck dares the viewer not only to see them but to recognize their presence still active within the American body politic.

CHAPTER 7

The Evolution of Mass-Killing

European Military Might: "Killing at a Distance"

Part 3 of the documentary opens with an animation of early humanity. The screen shows the great migrations out of Africa, rippling across the Middle East, into Asia, Europe, and eventually to the Pacific Islands and the Americas. The narration reminds us that Africa is the origin of all human life—that migration is not foreign to us; it is our beginning. Civilizations rise, languages form, agriculture develops, and societies take shape. With each step forward, humanity accomplishes wonders. But alongside progress also come conflict, division, and the pursuit of power.

The screen shifts again, now bearing the bold title: "Killing at a Distance." The phrase feels surgical, cold—yet precise. It encapsulates the transformation of war and conquest from hand-to-hand battle to detached, long-range slaughter, made possible by technological advancement and imperial ambition.

Raoul Peck turns our attention to the Mughal Empire, which rose to prominence in the early 16th century, around 1526. The Mughals, descendants of Central Asian warriors and Persian nobility, established a powerful and advanced Islamic civilization in South Asia. They were culturally refined, architecturally brilliant, and militarily formidable. But their Achilles heel was naval power. The Mughals, like many great land-based empires, had no formidable navy. They lacked ships equipped to carry heavy cannons or to project power over oceans.

To fill that gap, the Mughals began to enter into alliances with European maritime powers, particularly the British and Dutch East India Companies. These companies, originally formed as joint-stock trading ventures, quickly evolved into private empires, possessing their own armies, navies, and colonial mandates. What began as service-for-hire was quickly transformed into subjugation-by-commerce, and ultimately military dominance.

This era marks the beginning of a strategic inversion: Asian empires like the Mughals, who had once been dominant, began to depend on European powers, who in turn used those relationships to expand their control over global trade, territory, and people.

Meanwhile, China, long considered the jewel of ancient civilization, chose a different path. Confident in the protection of its borders—both natural and manmade—China saw little need to pursue naval dominance. While they had already invented gunpowder centuries earlier and had cast some of the world's first cannons, they saw no imminent threat requiring a vast fleet or a military-industrial expansion. That decision would later leave them vulnerable.

Europe, on the other hand, pursued armament with unmatched zeal. Gunpowder, cannon-casting, and metallurgy were refined. Cannons became more mobile. Gun barrels were rifled. Steel began to shape both weapons and the means to produce them. Killing at a distance was no longer theoretical—it was a technological reality.

As Raoul's narration continues, the documentary shows maps of trade routes overlaid with images of early muskets and flintlocks, sent to what Europeans called "third world territories"—a term revealing the hierarchy they imposed. These early firearms, slow to load and cumbersome to use, still marked a shift in global warfare. In many regions of Africa, Asia, and the Americas, these weapons represented both opportunity and subjugation: opportunity for defense, subjugation through dependence.

The documentary carefully illustrates the disparity in firepower. European countries were now mass-producing weapons, particularly those made from tempered steel, using industrial methods and financial backing from monarchs and merchants alike. African nations, though rich in culture and political structures, lacked the means to produce steel-based arms at scale. Their weaponry, often hand-forged and locally sourced, was no match for mass-imported European rifles and artillery.

The disparity wasn't just about weapons—it was about systems of production, capital, and imperial machinery. The conquest of land was now reinforced by the conquest of time and technology. Europeans had not only the guns, but also the factories, the ships, and the economic engines to sustain prolonged warfare, all while exporting these tools of violence under the guise of trade, religion, or civilization.

By the late 19th century, European weaponry had evolved from matchlock muskets to breech-loading rifles, Gatling guns, and rapid-fire artillery. The effectiveness of these technologies was tragically demonstrated in conflicts such as the Zulu Wars, the Opium Wars, and numerous anti-colonial uprisings that were swiftly crushed by European imperial forces. This superiority in arms allowed small imperial garrisons to subjugate entire regions, often outnumbered but never outgunned.

This section of the documentary makes clear: colonization was not merely ideological or economic—it was militarized. And the ability to "kill at a distance" became both a symbol and a strategy. It allowed the colonizer to destroy without seeing, to dominate without engaging, to dehumanize without touching.

This is the brutal arithmetic of empire!

The screen then shows the continent of Africa, the shape of it stark and massive against the background. A red highlight pulses over Sudan, narrowing in on the city of Omdurman. The year appears on the screen: 1898.

British Execution: A Structure of Violence

A voiceover explains that this was the moment when British imperial power would test itself against a numerically superior African resistance. The Mahdist army, named after their Islamic leader known as the Mahdi, had unified large parts of Sudan and held strong convictions rooted in faith and sovereignty. But in the eyes of the British Empire, they were not seen as a legitimate political or spiritual force—they were seen as "fanatics," "savages," and "brutes." Words used to justify what would follow.

Among the British troops was a young officer and war correspondent named Winston Churchill, who would later become one of the most famous figures of the 20th century. But here, in Omdurman, he was just another imperial soldier, armed not just with a gun but with a pen that knew how to flatter conquest and write it into history.

Churchill described the Sudanese defenders as "dervishes," and wrote in chilling detachment of the massacre that followed. He stated, "It was not a battle, but an execution… It was a matter of killing as many as possible in the shortest time." In his words, the slaughter was not a shame—it was strategy, efficiency, progress.

More than 11,000 Sudanese Mahdists were killed, many armed only with swords and spears. Fewer than 50 British soldiers died. The British had Maxim guns, rapid-firing weapons capable of mowing down waves of human bodies from a safe distance. The Sudanese had courage and conviction—but no firepower to match. And yet, the British called this a battle. A victory. A sign of civilization triumphing over barbarism.

The documentary presses the viewer to recognize that this was not merely an isolated event—it was an imperial pattern, driven by deep ideological fuel. The violence at Omdurman was not a last resort. It was a premeditated demonstration of technological supremacy, rooted in the belief that white, Christian, European power was destined to rule over darker-skinned peoples.

This is where ideologies like Manifest Destiny and the "White Man's Burden" quietly undergird the narrative. Though Manifest Destiny is primarily associated with American expansionism, its spirit echoed throughout European imperialism: the belief that certain nations were divinely appointed to bring civilization, by force, if necessary, to the rest of the world. The British, much like the Americans, clothed conquest in the garments of righteousness.

The notion of the "White Man's Burden," made famous by Rudyard Kipling just one year after Omdurman in 1899, preached that it was the moral duty of the West to civilize the "uncivilized," to govern the "childlike races" of the world. But beneath this paternalistic language lay brutality, domination, and slaughter, Omdurman being a prime example.

So, while British generals recorded victory and Churchill sharpened his pen, thousands of African bodies were buried in the sands of Sudan—not because they lacked bravery, but because they lacked cannons. This was not a fair fight. It was the ritual of colonial domination, dressed in military parade and righteous prose.

The documentary asks viewers not to simply see this as history, but to understand it as a structure of violence, backed by governments, celebrated by empires, and justified by philosophies that saw some humans as expendable and others as ordained.

The Militarization of American Industry

While there were wars of conquest overseas—across the continent of Africa, in Asia, and throughout the so-called New World—the industrial development of firearms was also shaping the path of colonization and imperialism within the United States. The documentary now narrows its lens to focus on the U.S. arms industry itself, a force that would not only shape domestic conquest but ultimately place the United States at the center of global power.

President George Washington, often lionized as the founder of the American Republic, played a central role in what would become the militarization of American industry. With the establishment of

Springfield Armory in 1794, Washington effectively jump-started the United States' state-sponsored weapons industry. Under his leadership, the federal government laid the foundation for what would become the world's first nationalized arms manufacturing complex. The Armory would eventually set the standard for mass production, precision machining, and interchangeable parts—all of which became defining features of industrial capitalism.

But this was not just about technological innovation. It was a vision: to arm a nation not just for defense, but for expansion. Guns would pave the frontier, subdue Indigenous resistance, and reinforce state power. Firearms became not only tools of war, but instruments of colonial enforcement, land seizure, and racial domination.

As the documentary unfolds, the screen presents an article headline: "The smoke of America's factory stacks is a signal of our workers' and employers' loyalty." In bold caps, a stark call to arms appears: "MORE GUNS, MORE SHIPS, MORE FOOD."

And beneath it, the message continues in regular type: "Our industries are the third and main supporting line of defense, our base of supplies. Without them, the Army and Navy would be helpless. As good patriots, let us strive to keep our industries strong."

This isn't just patriotic rhetoric—it reflects the deeply ingrained philosophy that war and industry are inseparable in the American experience. The United States, unlike many nations, fused capitalism with militarism, and that fusion became the economic engine of empire.

The screen shifts again—flickering through the faces of U.S. presidents: Ronald Reagan and his Vice President, then President George H.W.

Bush, then George W. Bush, Jimmy Carter, and Donald Trump. These are not simply leaders of political administrations—they are figureheads in a long lineage of military-industrial stewardship. Each continued policies that maintained or expanded America's global dominance through military buildup, defense contracting, and ideological justification.

The documentary then lists a series of military strategists and defense industry leaders whose influence shaped U.S. policy: Norman R. Augustine (former CEO of Lockheed Martin), Dov S. Zakheim (former Under Secretary of Defense), James G. Roche, Dick Cheney, John C. Rood, Francis J. Harvey—each a key architect in the infrastructure of perpetual war.

Animated imagery now shows fiery explosions—dated from 1798 through 1800, referencing the Quasi-War between the United States and France. But these early conflicts were only the beginning. The screen then becomes a whirlwind of timelines, marking war after war, theater after theater: from the Barbary Wars to the Mexican-American War, the Philippine-American War, World Wars, and countless interventions in Central and South America, Africa, the Middle East, and Southeast Asia. The list becomes too long to recite in full, but the point is made clear: war has become an industry, and the United States its most prolific manufacturer.

The Monroe Doctrine

It is within this context that the documentary presents the so-called Monroe Doctrine, introduced in 1823. President James Monroe, in his address to Congress, warned European powers to stay out of the affairs of the Western Hemisphere. While framed as a protective doctrine meant to guard the sovereignty of newly independent Latin American nations, in practice, it served another purpose. It established U.S. hegemony over the Americas, asserting the nation's right to intervene, influence, and dominate the affairs of its neighbors.

What began as rhetoric became practice. From the annexation of Texas to the overthrow of governments in Guatemala (1954), Chile (1973), and the long list of U.S.-backed military regimes and covert interventions, the Monroe Doctrine evolved into a justification for regional empire—a colonialism of the hemisphere, draped in stars and stripes.

The doctrine, alongside Manifest Destiny, revealed the American mindset: not merely of independence, but of entitlement. Entitlement to control land, people, and markets. And behind every ideology, every political doctrine stood the arms industry—a machine that profited from conquest, that mechanized killing, that converted blood into capital.

What the documentary compels us to understand is that the industrialization of death, from Springfield Armory to Silicon Valley drone warfare, is not a deviation from American identity—it is part of its foundation.

Here's a troubling thought to ponder: *Without war, the machine would stall. But without conscience, the machine will never stop.*

Atomic Destruction: "Dealing With the Animal."

On the screen: "Leaving the Atlantic behind, America's reach became global."

A textual overlay names Reverend Josiah Strong and his bestselling 1885 text, "Our Country." A quote appears: "As a superior race, the United States had a divine responsibility to control the world."

Peck uses Strong's ideology to signal America's shift—from isolation to global dominance, from Manifest Destiny to manifest empire. This was white supremacist theology in policy form. He then pivots sharply to a darker chapter in modern warfare: August 1945, Hiroshima. Nagasaki.

Peck's language is unflinching: this was not a military necessity; it was a massacre. Hundreds of thousands—civilians, women, children—were incinerated by atomic bombs. And yet, the act was heralded as decisive, heroic, even righteous. Raoul challenges this narrative. Was Hiroshima truly a "war crime?" Would it be called so—if the power to name the event lay elsewhere?

To underscore the moral horror, he deploys a metaphor: "Imagine a chess match where the king is the emperor. We protect the king. Everyone else becomes collateral damage." That is Hiroshima: "a calculated blow determined by algorithm," executed at distance, killing innocent people who had no warning, no defense—just as in Omdurman and other colonial slaughter.

Peck plays a clip of President Harry S. Truman, responding to a religious plea for mercy. Truman said, "The only language they understand is the one we've been using to bombard them. When you have to deal with an animal, you have to treat it as an animal. It is most regrettable, but nonetheless true."

Peck then exclaimed: *"EXTERMINATE ALL THE BRUTES!"* This title lifted from both history and the documentary's own call to conscience—

to recognize that genocidal ideologies have always been marketed as national duty, whether at Omdurman, on battlefields, or over the cities of Hiroshima and Nagasaki.

The screen now shifts to horrific images of Hiroshima and Nagasaki in the wake of atomic destruction. Buildings reduced to skeletal remains. Ashes. Rubble. Fields of devastation—block after block, leveled. Structures that once held life, commerce, and culture are now flattened, unrecognizable.

Bodies are seen lying in the streets, others scorched by the heat from the blast. The scars of this tragedy are visible—burned flesh, permanent injuries, evidence of human suffering caused by an act that cannot be undone. These are the visible results of the atomic bombs dropped in August 1945. The destruction is total! The damage is irreversible!

Raoul Peck presents these images not as spectacle, but as indictment. He calls the act what it was: not a heroic act, but a massacre—a premeditated annihilation of civilian life, justified by political and military powers, carried out at a distance.

Peck draws attention to the ideology behind this action. The atomic bomb, he argues, was not merely dropped to end war—it was a tool of imperial assertion. The decision to bomb was rooted in a belief system that allowed its executors to define who counted as human and who could be sacrificed.

The statement presented by President Harry S. Truman: "When you have to deal with a beast, you have to treat him as a beast." This chilling account is connected to the racial logic of dehumanization. In the eyes of those in power, the Japanese were not considered equals—they were labeled as "animals," and such language made their destruction more palatable, more acceptable to the American public, and less likely to be questioned as a moral crime.

Peck then poses a profound question: Why wasn't this called a war crime?

And the answer he offers is as disturbing as it is revealing: Those who have the power to name events, to define history, will name it in ways that protect their interests and shield them from accountability. It is in this context that Peck reaffirms the central thesis of his work: "Exterminate all the brutes."

The phrase is no longer merely a reference to colonial Africa or the Americas—it becomes a global principle of domination. The same logic that justified the conquest of Omdurman, the enslavement of Africans, and the genocide of Native Americans is the logic that authorized the dropping of atomic bombs on civilian cities.

Through these images and words, Raoul Peck underscores the core truth: Brutality is not accidental in history; it is foundational. And until that foundation is confronted and dismantled, the violence will not only continue—it will be renamed, justified, and repeated.

Ndugu M'Hali

From the graphic image of a Japanese man whose body is severely burned—flesh scarred, skin mangled by the atomic bombs dropped on Hiroshima and Nagasaki—the documentary abruptly transitions. It cuts to another scene, now in black and white. Presented are archival photographs. Utilizing these photos, Peck, as the photographer of the scenes, performs a symbolic reenactment.

In these composed images, a European man, referred to only as Henry, stands beside a young African child, labeled only as "boy." The composition is staged—constructed, not spontaneous. This is a symbolic act directed by Peck to reflect the colonial narrative of domination, objectification, and racialized display.

Peck narrates, giving instructions for the photograph to be taken. The white man stands upright in explorer's garb, clutching a rifle. The young boy stands shirtless, wrapped in cloth, also holding a weapon. Behind them, a painted backdrop imitates jungle foliage, with stones and vegetation added to create the illusion of an imperial conquest setting.

This colonial vignette reveals more than a posed photo. It's a statement. Peck uses this image to underscore the exportation of Africans, the imposition of European mythologies, and what he also refers to as "killing at a distance." Here, it is not only physical death, but a killing of identity, history, and human dignity. The photo session becomes a performance of conquest—one where Africans are made to pose in submission, stripped of name, history, and voice.

The screen then presents: Henry Morton Stanley and Kalulu, 1872. The boy, who was originally named Ndugu M'Hali, had his identity renamed by Stanley to Kalulu. Peck, narrating in the voice of the boy, says: "He changed my name to Kalulu. He said it sounded better." This simple line underscores the invasive colonial mindset—that even the sound of a name must be made to please the ear of the oppressor. The theft is not only of body, but of culture and self.

We Are Not a Footnote

Following this, the screen shifts to actual images from Raoul Peck's life. We see childhood photos—him with his family—portraits of a boy growing into manhood across borders and cultures. He reflects on how his parents raised him with discipline, resilience, and a clear understanding that education would be his most powerful weapon. He was trained to be both a good learner and a good soldier, navigating a world where his Blackness would constantly be interrogated and diminished by those who saw themselves as racially superior.

Peck's reflection here is deeply personal, but also representative. His experiences—particularly when he moved to Europe—exposed him to a more subtle, but no less violent, form of racism: one that did not strike the body, but sought to disarm the spirit. Earlier in this documentary, he speaks of how, as a child, he once viewed white people as extended family. But adulthood revealed a different truth—one where he was not seen as equal, but as a supporting character, a footnote in a grand Western narrative.

In Peck's view, the white gaze sees the Black or Brown figure as expendable. As he narrates, the Black character is the one killed off early in the film—never meant to be the hero, never meant to survive to the end. It is a powerful metaphor for the psychological and cultural erasure endured by colonized peoples around the globe.

Peck's confrontation with this reality, especially in Europe, was not marked by a physical altercation, but by something far more insidious: a systematic denial of personhood, a world where Black life is made small, muted, and irrelevant. It is not that the world did not see him; it is that it refused to acknowledge his full humanity.

This sequence is Raoul Peck's visual meditation on displacement, renaming, and survival. It is also a call to remember that behind every photograph, behind every name change, and behind every erased history, there is a person. A soul. A life—too often reduced to a prop in someone else's story. But we are not a footnote, we are the very authors of history, the keepers of memory, and the voices that refuse to be silent.

Heart of Darkness

Raoul now gives attention to Joseph Conrad's book, Heart of Darkness, a novel often referenced in discussions of imperial conquest and the psychological violence embedded in colonization. Conrad's portrayal of the Congo exposes not only the brutality of European imperialism but also the descent into moral and spiritual decay that accompanies unchecked domination. The jungle, in Conrad's narrative, becomes the stage upon which the façade of European civility is stripped away, revealing the barbarism at the heart of so-called enlightenment.

This literary reference connects seamlessly to the historical truths Raoul presents. As the screen transitions, images appear depicting the ruthless exploitation of Africa by European powers—ivory, gold, rubber—ripped from the earth and the hands of African laborers. Colonizers left no resource untouched, no life unscarred. This new era of imperial expansion ushered in an even more sinister age of racism. As Raoul explains, Europeans began to mistake their military dominance for intellectual and even biological superiority. What had once been masked by the rhetoric of civilization and commerce now became open, unrestrained racial ideology. No one had to pretend anymore. This was domination, raw and unapologetic.

A stage photographer appears next on the screen, operating in the Congo. He arranges his subjects not for art, but for propaganda. The words "Rubber Plantation, Congo, 1904" appear, grounding this moment in historical specificity. The photograph that follows is not symbolic or staged—it is real, and it is clear. Two European colonizers stand with composed authority. Beside them are three African figures. Two of the Africans hold human hands—severed from the bodies of unknown victims. These mutilated hands are not anomalies. They are proof!

Under King Leopold II's rule in the Congo Free State, such horrors were routine. Mutilation, amputation, and execution were methods used to enforce rubber quotas. The logic was simple and inhuman: if a bullet was used, it had to be accounted for. Severed hands were the proof.

This image is a visual indictment of colonial violence. It exposes the lie of benevolent imperialism and strips away any illusion that colonization was about uplift or progress. The Congo was not a blank slate for European ambition—it was a land invaded, its people brutalized, its resources pillaged. The photograph confirms what Conrad's fiction could only suggest: the true heart of darkness was not in the jungle, but in the empire that claimed to civilize it.

Through this moment in the documentary, Raoul draws a direct line from literary metaphor to lived atrocity. The connection between ideology and action is made visible. The camera doesn't flinch, and neither does the truth.

The scene shifts to Europe—likely Rome—where Raoul Peck shares more of his personal story. Footage of his family appears once again, grounding the narrative in his lived experiences. He recalls a statement made by a

President of the United States about Western civilization and its will to survive. But Peck reflects honestly—he never felt part of Western civilization. Though he had lived in places shaped by its systems and values, he did not see himself included in its identity or legacy.

He recounts a memory from his youth: a curiosity he had toward joining the Boy Scouts. As a young man, despite his weariness of Western institutions, especially those with strong religious influence, Peck, as a child, had an interest in the organization. His white friend, Robert, was very involved in its practices. Robert introduced Peck to elements of the Scouts—showing him the various hand signs, how to tie knots, and other things associated with Scout activity.

Peck then introduces the figure of Robert Baden-Powell, the founder of the Boy Scouts. He notes that during the Second Ashanti War in 1896, Baden-Powell was sent as part of a British military envoy to seize King Prempeh I of the Ashanti. The conquest took place without a single shot being fired.

Peck explains that this was a disappointment to Baden-Powell, who had hoped for a military engagement to showcase his command and to receive military honors. Nevertheless, the Ashanti king and his entire family were taken captive, but the king and his mother were made to bow before their British captors.

This section reveals the deeper connection between celebrated Western institutions and their colonial origins. The Boy Scouts, often viewed as a symbol of discipline and civic development, are here placed in their proper historical context—founded by a man whose military service was directly linked to the expansion of empire and the subjugation of African sovereignty. The capture of King Prempeh was not simply a tactical event; it represented the broader project of European imperial control over African peoples and resources.

Peck's reflections remind viewers that even familiar institutions often carry legacies of domination and conquest. By connecting personal memory with historical reality, the documentary continues to challenge what many take for granted—and to expose the colonial roots woven into the fabric of modern global life.

The visual now provides an African woman, who is shown tending to the interior of a colonial outpost. The unsettling calm is then interrupted by the arrival of the "white man"—an embodiment of imperial entitlement and white supremacy. His slow disrobing and the woman's forced participation in bathing him were not just a scene of physical domination, but symbolic of the sexual and racial hierarchies imposed by colonialism. Her blank, somber stare is not just a sign of submission, but of emotional detachment and silent resistance. The act is not consensual servitude—it is coerced compliance under occupation and powerlessness.

Outside, distant weeping and singing punctuate the silence. The camera lingers on her gaze, now turned outward. Through the window, she sees four African men hanging lifeless from a tree—lynched by colonial enforcers or loyal agents of imperial terror. The sound of mourning, carried in song by unseen women, fills the air like a dirge. She turns her head, slowly, deliberately, back toward the "white man," who still sits arrogantly in the tub. Her gaze is no longer blank—it's filled with disdain, grief, and a deep, wordless accusation.

The "white man," meanwhile, meets her eyes with a look that borders on smugness or dull indifference—perhaps confused, perhaps contemptuous, but certainly unaware or unmoved by the suffering around him. His comfort and his clean body contrast violently with the mutilated, lifeless Black bodies outside the window.

This scene powerfully conveys the intersection of racial violence, exploitation, and the psychological toll of colonialism. It encapsulates the horror of a system in which Black bodies are used, discarded, or destroyed to preserve white power and comfort. The African woman's silence is louder than any words—it carries the unbearable weight of resistance, sorrow, and survival. The distant mourning connects the private violence inside the home to the communal grief outside, drawing a line from personal humiliation to collective trauma.

The scene does not offer resolution—it indicts. It holds a mirror to the past and demands the viewer reflect on the cost of empire, not in abstraction, but in the intimate, unbearable realities of the colonized.

CHAPTER 8

Muséum National d'Histoire Naturelle: Weaponizing Evolution Theory

The screen then shifts, presenting breathtaking footage of the city of Paris, its architecture, its movement, and its beauty—only to land at the doors of the Muséum National d'Histoire Naturelle, the National Museum of Natural History. The narration transitions with the name Georges Cuvier, a figure whose work left a powerful impact on the 18th and 19th centuries.

Known as the father of paleontology, Cuvier gave a compelling speech that captivated listeners as he introduced the radical idea that animals could become extinct. This concept, now fundamental to modern biology, was unsettling to many in his era. Until then, extinction was unthinkable, as it contradicted the prevailing notion of divine design and permanence in creation.

As Peck continues, the year 1850 appears on the screen, and the name Herbert Spencer emerges. Spencer was an English philosopher who popularized the term "survival of the fittest," a phrase that would soon become a philosophical foundation for social Darwinism. Peck points to a chilling quote from Spencer: "If they are not sufficiently complete to live, they die, and it is best they should die."

Spencer openly applied the logic of natural selection and extinction not just to animals, but to human races, arguing that "inferior races" were naturally being removed from the earth. This thinking would become a dangerous ideological tool—weaponizing evolutionary theory to justify colonization, conquest, slavery, and systemic genocide.

By linking Georges Cuvier and Herbert Spencer, Peck highlights a grim evolution in Western scientific thought. Cuvier, while grounded in empirical observation, laid a foundation for thinking in categories of extinction. Spencer distorted that foundation by applying it to hierarchies among people, treating cultural and racial groups as biologically unequal and expendable. This scientific veneer gave imperialism a new justification—not only was it the right of the strong to rule, it was nature's way.

Peck then introduces the name Robert Knox, a Scottish anatomist whose racial theories further entrenched these ideas in 19th-century thinking. Knox argued that race was the single most important factor in determining human capability, morality, and worth. He insisted that racial characteristics were fixed, immutable, and inherently unequal. He wrote in The Races of Men: "Race is everything: literature, science, art—in a word, civilization depends on it."

Knox's work helped provide an intellectual framework for colonial powers to claim that African, Asian, and Indigenous peoples were not just culturally inferior, but biologically so. His assertions gave scientific cover for oppression, for the denial of sovereignty, and for the brutal violence that followed. These men—Cuvier, Spencer, and Knox—represent the transformation of science into ideological weaponry.

By placing their names in sequence, Peck exposes how the language of science was corrupted into a rationale for dehumanization, an essential part of the machinery of empire. Their theories shaped minds, policies, and empires. They made the genocide of peoples seem not only necessary, but natural.

Mount Rushmore: A Contradiction

As the documentary continues, a montage appears—images of people from across the world: men and women of all ethnicities and backgrounds. One striking image lingers—a Native American woman, her face adorned with traditional paint, looking directly into the lens. It is a moment of dignity and rooted identity. But this reverent image is abruptly replaced. The screen cuts sharply to footage of Mount Rushmore, that colossal monument carved into the sacred Black Hills of South Dakota.

The contradiction is immediate and intentional. For the Lakota Sioux, the Black Hills are not simply a region—they are holy ground, land stolen in violation of treaties by the U.S. government, particularly the 1868 Fort Laramie Treaty, which had guaranteed these lands to the Lakota in perpetuity. The carving of Mount Rushmore into these sacred hills is viewed by many Indigenous people not as a tribute to democracy, but as *a symbol of conquest and desecration.*

Even more troubling is the choice of the figures memorialized: George Washington, Thomas Jefferson, Theodore Roosevelt, and Abraham Lincoln—each representing, in varying degrees, the expansion of the

American empire, and the displacement, removal, or erasure of Native peoples. For the Lakota Sioux and other Native communities, the monument is a stark reminder of the violence and betrayal they have endured under the banner of American exceptionalism.

Raoul Peck then connects the dots through narration, tying back to the ideological foundation of these contradictions. He invokes President Thomas Jefferson, one of the figures etched into Rushmore, quoting his disbelief that a single species could disappear from nature. Jefferson's thoughts reflect a worldview in which extinction—of animals, of peoples, of cultures—was seen as inconceivable, unnatural, and even impossible.

And yet, Jefferson's own policies and views on race and land contributed directly to the dispossession and attempted erasure of entire peoples. His Indian Removal policies, as previously mentioned, laid the groundwork for the eventual Trail of Tears, and he also profited from slavery, while philosophizing about liberty.

This moment in the film draws a straight line from the earlier section of the documentary, where Herbert Spencer had compared extinction to the removal of "inferior races" from the earth, and Robert Knox declared that race determined all civilization. Here, Peck builds on that theme: not only did scientific racism provide a framework to justify colonialism, but the very leaders enshrined in national monuments embraced ideologies that normalized conquest and rationalized the extinction of peoples as historical inevitability—or worse, as divine design.

The irony deepens. Jefferson, who once thought extinction unthinkable, is now immortalized in a monument built atop sacred land, honoring a legacy of expansion that directly contributed to the erasure of Native cultures. Mount Rushmore thus becomes not just a contradiction—but a symbol of historical amnesia. It enshrines men who helped build a nation by denying others the right to exist freely in their own land.

Then, the documentary makes yet another striking visual shift. The screen now fills with images of animals—elephants and antelope galloping across grasslands, birds soaring through skies, schools of fish weaving through coral reefs beneath the sea. Life teems across every element of the earth—land, air, and ocean. These scenes remind the viewer of the vastness, the fragility, and the interwoven beauty of the natural world. During the display of the vastness of creatures, Peck mentions that "99% of all species have died out."

Suddenly, the imagery transforms into a sweeping bird's-eye view of the entire planet, a vision of Earth from above, slowly rotating in space. Juxtaposed with this cosmic view, we see the image of a modern car, inexplicably orbiting the planet, with a lone driver wearing a space suit—his hands on the wheel, as if navigating not just through traffic, but through the very trajectory of human history.

Raoul Peck's narration quietly declares: "This is the scope of our story." In this final moment of the sequence, Peck is not only summarizing what the viewer has witnessed but pointing to the scale of human impact and the ideological reach of colonialism, racism, and conquest.

The story is not only about what happened on the ground—in Africa, in the Americas, or in Europe—but about how far-reaching the consequences have become. From the desecration of sacred lands to the extinction of species, from scientific racism to the mythology carved into mountains, from human atrocities to space-age absurdities—the documentary asks us to confront a legacy that has reached planetary proportions.

The driver in the space suit becomes a symbol of humanity in the modern age: technologically advanced, self-assured, and yet lost in orbit, disconnected from the very Earth that sustains him. Peck is challenging the viewer not just to see the past, but to question where this trajectory ends—and whether our collective story will continue along this same course of domination, or whether a new direction can be imagined.

This is the story we must reckon with.

Pseudoscience and Survival of the Fittest

The scene once again shifts as it portrays survival of the fittest. Animals are shown engaged in fierce combat—fighting for territory, fighting for food—while weaker animals fall prey. These striking images are juxtaposed with narration that introduces Charles Darwin. Raoul Peck notes that Darwin, as a young student, had been exposed to the controversial lectures of Robert Knox. Darwin would go on to publish his landmark work on the Origin of Species in 1859, where he outlined the principle that species adapt to their environment through a process he called natural selection.

Raoul uses this moment to trace how Darwin's scientific ideas, though not explicitly about human society, would later be used to justify racial hierarchies. Peck makes clear that Darwin's theories became particularly useful in spreading racist ideology.

The images that now appear on screen reinforce this point—depictions of European scientists and anthropologists measuring the heads, noses, and facial angles of people from various ethnic groups. These were not neutral scientific studies, but part of a broader enterprise meant to categorize and rank human beings by supposed racial value.

Peck then asserts that Darwin's input made it easier for imperialists to embrace the genocide of what they called "inferior peoples." This wasn't science in pursuit of truth—it was science weaponized in service of conquest. The camera lingers on these pseudo-scientific practices, reinforcing how easily knowledge can be distorted when it is pressed into the service of power.

By placing Darwin's theory alongside visual documentation of racial measurement and classification, the documentary does not critique the science itself as much as it critiques the misuse of that science. These ideas became embedded in the machinery of colonial rule, providing moral and intellectual cover for acts of unspeakable cruelty.

In this way, Peck continues to build his argument: that the violence of colonization was never just physical—it was ideological, it was philosophical, and it was falsely made to appear rational, even natural. That is the legacy of how Darwin's theory was interpreted and applied—not in scientific journals, but in the real-world policies and brutal systems that defined the age of empire.

Raoul continues with a chilling assertion: genocide became the inevitable product of progress. It was not simply an accidental consequence—it was the logical outgrowth of the ideologies that defined imperial expansion and colonial domination. The belief in progress, when fused with racial hierarchy and pseudoscientific thinking, made genocide not only conceivable but necessary in the eyes of those who saw themselves as civilizers of the world. It became a mechanism to clear the land, secure resources, and eliminate resistance from so-called inferior peoples.

Peck explains that once Charles Darwin's ideas were appropriated and distorted, they gave moral and intellectual cover to acts of mass violence. After Darwin's input, it became easier for imperialists to rationalize genocide. If nature selected the strong to survive, then man—especially white European man—had a duty to eliminate the weak. Those who refused to embrace these ideologies, who pushed back against the rising tide of *scientific racism*, were not seen as courageous dissenters. They were instead labeled as backwards, irrational, or uneducated. In the name of reason and modernity, their resistance was mocked or silenced.

As this powerful commentary unfolds, the screen presents a stark visual: Former Munitions Factory, Union Werke, Auschwitz. The shift is immediate and jarring. Auschwitz—the site of industrialized death, a name now synonymous with mechanized genocide—stands as a grim reminder of where these ideologies led. The same factories that once produced weapons, now become emblematic of a system capable of annihilating millions. What began as conquest and colonization had returned home in the most horrifying form imaginable.

By invoking Auschwitz, Raoul Peck draws a straight line from the ideological roots of imperialism to the Holocaust. The racial pseudoscience used to justify the slaughter of Congolese, Indigenous peoples, and enslaved Africans had been refined, systematized, and repatriated to Europe. The genocide of Jews, Roma, and others under Nazi rule was not an aberration—it was a culmination. A mirror held up to a Western world that had long practiced extermination abroad under other names: *civilization, order, progress.*

Peck's narration is not merely a historical analysis—it is a confrontation! A demand that we stop seeing genocide as the work of mere monsters and instead recognize it as the legacy of policies, philosophies, and institutions embraced and enforced by powerful nations in the name of modernity.

Peck adds to his narration a quote from Darwin, "Regarding future life, each person will have to judge for himself."

CHAPTER 9

Savage, Semi-Civilized and Civilized

A European man, in a creative reenactment, is shown standing in a grand lecture hall. His presence is formal and commanding, as if presiding over a moment of great intellectual and cultural consequence. The screen presents the words: London, 1866. He addresses the audience with an air of confidence, announcing a time of profound transformation, "light overcoming darkness." This phrase captures the ideological spirit of the 19th century, when European powers believed their domination marked progress, enlightenment, and destiny.

With a solemn gesture, the speaker introduces the man of the hour: Dr. Frederic Farrar, a prominent theologian and thinker of his time. As Farrar steps forward in this staged reenactment, he begins a lecture drawn directly from historical rhetoric—words that would reinforce the foundations of racial hierarchy and justify colonialism under the guise of science and morality.

Farrar begins by referencing the work of the famed Swedish botanist, Carl Linnaeus, stating: "The great Swedish botanist Carl Linnaeus discriminates with his unusual acuteness the intellectual and moral characteristics of four great human families: Homo Americanus, Homo Europaeus, Homo Asiaticus, and Homo Afer."

Linnaeus, best known for his scientific classification of plants and animals, also categorized human beings into racial types—assigning characteristics to each based on European assumptions of superiority. These so-called "families" were not neutral or objective categories, but deeply biased projections used to bolster European self-image.

Farrar continues, explaining that these four human types could be reduced into three essential divisions: *savage, semi-civilized, and civilized.* As he makes this declaration, he gestures toward a white marble sculpture of a European man, clearly intended to embody the ideal of civilization. Farrar boldly asserts that only the Aryan and Semitic races are truly civilized, while the rest are consigned to the margins of human development.

The lecture's tone is didactic and paternalistic, delivered as if an uncontested truth. But as this creative reenactment continues, the camera shifts away from the 19th-century setting. It slowly pans across a modern audience—diverse in race, background, and gender—watching the staged performance unfold. The expressions on their faces tell a different story. They do not sit as passive listeners. Instead, there is discomfort, disbelief, and a silent protest in their demeanor.

The contrast between the past and present is striking. This diverse modern audience, seated in solemn silence, becomes a mirror to us—the viewers—challenging us to confront the deeply rooted ideologies that once paraded as science and theology. Their facial expressions loudly exclaim: How dare you exalt one race as inherently superior? How dare you dismiss the civilizations and cultures of non-European peoples?

This moment is more than just a reflection of outdated beliefs; it is a vivid demonstration of how the foundations of racial hierarchy were laid with the full endorsement of religion, science, and Western academia. Linnaeus's taxonomy, though scientific in form, was infused with a racial agenda. Farrar's sermon-like lecture reveals how the language of faith and scholarship merged to elevate whiteness and relegate other races to categories of savagery or incompleteness.

Peck's use of reenactment here is not embellishment – it is exposé. The visual technique forces the audience to reckon with the ideologies that shaped colonization and empire, not just through wars and economic conquest, but through textbooks, sermons, lectures, and museum displays.

By merging the 19th-century rhetoric with the watchful eyes of a 21st-century audience, Peck delivers a sharp and intentional juxtaposition: the enduring presence of racial ideology in the fabric of the West. This reenacted lecture becomes a powerful indictment—not simply of what was said in 1866, but of how those ideas still echo in our institutions and social structures today.

The scene continues with Dr. Farrar parading himself as the embodiment of arrogance and racial superiority, maintaining the belief that whiteness is the pinnacle of human development. With theatrical flair and chilling conviction, he continues to make false and degrading assertions about the supposed supremacy of the white race over all others.

Then, in a moment that shocks both the fictional and viewing audiences, the documentary shows Farrar walking over to a gurney stationed beside his podium. He forcefully removes the white sheet that covers the body of a deceased man of African descent. With cold detachment, Farrar looks at the man's body and declares him the "least of all uncivilized creatures." The air in the room thickens. The audience gasps, horrified by the spectacle. Disbelief and disgust spread across the room like wildfire.

In a surge of emotion, an audience member—representing a modern-day European—rises in protest, yelling in German: "How dare you think your heritage is better than mine!" The voice is filled with rage and sorrow. He swears at Farrar and storms out of the lecture hall. Others soon follow. What had once been a silent and attentive audience is now a crowd in uproar. Shouts erupt. Some curse the speaker. Many shake their heads in disbelief.

The lecture has transformed into a battlefield—not of swords, but of ideology and identity. Concern and unease are visible in the faces of those who organized this presentation. But Farrar, undeterred and consumed by his disdain for non-white peoples, continues. He shouts into the crowd, clinging to his doctrine of supremacy, while spewing his mantra: "Irreclaimable are the savages."

Then, as a haunting symbol of scientific dehumanization, a European man dressed in full white attire—with a white cap and white mask—quietly pushes an empty gurney down a long, dim hallway. The wheels echo in the corridor as the chilling voice of Farrar rings out again in the distance, repeating: "Irreclaimable savages! Irreclaimable savages!"

It is at this moment that Peck interjects with a profound question: "What actually happened when knowledge, industry, and enlightenment exterminated the inferior races?" This question lingers as the scene transitions.

Peck reflects on Darwin—not as a neutral scientist, but as a man who traveled through South America in his youth and witnessed horrors with his own eyes. Raoul reminds us that Darwin saw General Rosas' soldiers in Argentina brutally butcher Indigenous people—how they were smeared in blood and vomit. He knew that eyes were gouged out when a captured Indian bit into a soldier's thumb and refused to release it. He knew of the systematic torture of women and the forced confessions of prisoners. Darwin had a term for this brutality: "The struggle for life."

Institutional Sterility and Racial Erasure

As Peck narrates these realities, we return to Jesup or the "white man," the character earlier seen bathing in the river and later being washed by the African woman. Now he appears in this new scene. No longer a symbol of colonial savagery in the past, Jesup is shown in black, semiformal modern-day attire, standing over a surgical table surrounded by cold, detached white-coated figures—men who resemble mad scientists, but whose demeanor suggests they are not simply researchers but agents of something more disturbing.

In the same room stands a Black man. He had been summoned by Jesup while attending the lecture. He is dressed in modern clothing, silently observing the white scientists who were standing by. He is calm, composed—but the weight of the moment is apparent. One of the white scientists approaches him and, with a cold gaze, asks his last name. The Black man returns the gaze unflinchingly and answers with clarity and steel in his voice: "Trouillot." The scientist then asks for his first name. Without hesitation, the man responds: "Rolph Michel."

In that moment, a deeper history surfaces. Rolph Michel Trouillot, the Haitian scholar, historian, and author, now stands symbolically as the subject of examination. Without a word from the white-coated men, he begins to remove his modern clothing, fully aware of what is about to happen. This is no accident. This is ritual. This is commentary.

Now partially unclothed, Trouillot stands upright, steady, defiant. His eyes never leave the face of Jesup, who approaches with a sleek, modern-looking medical device. Jesup asks, "Are you ready?" With resolve, Trouillot responds, "Sure."

Jesup raises the device and places it on Trouillot's forehead. A sharp mechanical sound is heard—the device activates. It lands like a death sentence. Trouillot collapses instantly to the ground, his body limp, as if executed not just by science, but by history. The same history now living in the present; the same racial supremacist ideology that in the past and presented earlier in the documentary, showing the "Indian" woman shot in the head with ease by the "white man," lives on.

Now, a new scene unfolds. One of the white-coated scientists—his face obscured by a mask—wheels Trouillot's lifeless body on a gurney down another hallway. The surroundings are dimly lit, cast in the pale hue of institutional sterility. The gurney rolls into a cold room. In this space lie dozens of bodies—perhaps 50 or more—of other Africans and non-white individuals who met the same fate. Each body lies covered, still, and silent. It is a chilling gallery of racial erasure.

Peck offers no direct commentary in this moment. The symbolism speaks for itself. The past has not passed—it merely changed its uniform. And now it seeks to rewrite, reclassify, and erase. However, Peck does offer the following: "Like Roxanne, like Michel-Rolph, like Sven... I do have my nightmares as well."

This scene is not just about conquest. It is about how science was used to justify the unspeakable. It is about how pseudoscience became law, how racism became data, and how human beings became experiments. It is about what happens when the intellectual legacy of white supremacy cloaks itself in objectivity—and why we must not forget.

Death Mills and Genocide

Now appearing on the screen are the words: "Death Mills, Billy Wilder, 1945." A haunting title introducing the grim aftermath of humanity's greatest engineered horrors. The screen follows with stark text: "Opening of the concentration camps." These visuals are not dramatizations—they are unfiltered records. Within these "death mills," history provides us with pictures of rows of skeletal bodies, hollow eyes, death by systematic machinery. The silence of these images screams louder than any narration ever could.

Raoul Peck now speaks—his voice subdued, reflective. He introduces a quote by Winston Churchill, as Britain confronted the atrocities uncovered in Nazi death camps: "We are in the presence of a crime without a name." Yet, Peck adds, this crime had already been described with the same reference but renamed. As early as 1943, a Polish-Jewish lawyer by the name of Raphael Lemkin had named it. Genocide. This renaming, the word Genocide now appears in bold capital letters across the screen. It is more than a term—it is a moral indictment against modern civilization.

Peck continues his narration, footage is now shown from inside the New York Public Library. He refers to the Raphael Lemkin Collection, citing precisely: Reel 3, Box 2, Folder 1. Within this archival document lies a sobering list—a chronicle of the world's genocides. A ledger of loss, betrayal, erasure.

Strategy of Domination

The screen transitions to a new title: "Modern Times." Then, slowly, one by one, each of the forty-one genocides listed in Lemkin's record flashes on the screen. The first genocide was named: "Genocide by the Germans against the Native Africans." A likely reference to the Herero and Namaqua genocide in what is today Namibia, carried out by the German Empire from 1904 to 1908, often regarded as the first genocide of the 20th century.

Each subsequent entry adds another chapter to this unending volume of annihilation. Genocide in the Congo. Genocide in Armenia. Genocide in Cambodia. Genocide in Rwanda. Genocide against Indigenous peoples in the Americas. And finally, the screen stops on the last entry: "Genocide against the Natives of Australia."

Then, the screen shifts tone. No longer presenting history by name or date, it now confronts the viewer with the vocabulary of destruction. One word at a time, each term imposed in bold white letters, one over another, overtaking the entire frame: **Enslaving. Killing. Dispossessing. Starving. Separating Families. Forcing Conversion. Re-Education.**

Each term is not just an action; it is an institution, a system, a strategy of domination. Prior to the screen pulses with these words, Peck overlays historical imagery. Drawings of imperial figures, depicted in biblical garb or classical postures, lead Indigenous populations into "submission" and so-called "enlightenment." These are not scenes of uplift; they are visual tools of justification. A false moral order imposed on cultures being dismantled.

Actual black-and-white photographs soon follow—Indigenous children, seated beside Christian missionaries, their expressions a mix of blank obedience and cultural disorientation. Elders standing beside colonial officers. Native People clothed in unfamiliar uniforms, their identities repurposed. These are not family portraits. They are records of forced assimilation. The camera becomes both witness and accomplice.

The words reappear—repeated again, in blinding white, multiplying, until they nearly blur together, becoming an overwhelming field of domination: ENSLAVING. KILLING. STARVING. RE-EDUCATION. CONVERSION.

Here, the documentary makes a definitive statement. *Genocide is not only the mass death of bodies—it is the obliteration of memory, culture, and selfhood.* It is erasure disguised as civilization. It is renaming a child. It is putting selected verses and perverted interpretations of the Holy Book in their hands while burning their language and their gods. It is the taking of land, the breaking of lineage, the turning of survivors into subjects.

Peck leaves no ambiguity. These crimes, now documented by Lemkin, now repeated on screen, are not isolated acts. They are structural. They are rationalized. They are codified. And for those who survived them, they were often photographed beside their captors, to prove that "order" and dominance had been established over the "brutes."

This moment in the documentary is not a climax, but a reckoning. It confronts viewers with the reality that genocide is not only the domain of tyrants, but of modern nations, of so-called "civilized" societies, of powers who viewed domination as destiny.

From the colonized child to the re-educated prisoner, from the forced convert to the disappeared elder—each word, each photo, each page from Lemkin's archive is an indictment not just of what happened, but of what was allowed to happen. And this is where Peck leaves the viewer—not with closure, but with a burden of knowledge. *These are the receipts of history!*

Chief Black Kettle and Medicine Woman Ar-no-ho-wok: Truce offered - Truce Denied

A new scene appears on the screen. It is an animation of a snowy wilderness—bleak, frigid, and hauntingly still. The air is thick with falling snow, carried sideways by a bitter wind. The screen displays the date: November 27, 1868, and the location: Washita River, "Indian Territory." Through the storm, two figures slowly emerge on horseback, pressing forward through the white haze. The animation presents their cultural adornment and weathered appearance against the wintery landscape.

Their names appear across the screen: Chief Black Kettle and Medicine Woman Ar-no-ho-wok. They ride together, hunched against the cold, wrapped in hides and blankets, making their way across the deep snow. The quiet rhythm of their horses' hooves is soon broken by a distant sound—hoofbeats. Many of them. Faint at first, then growing louder, thunderous, approaching from beyond the curtain of white.

As they reach the edge of the Washita River, the pair stops. The wind whips around them. The horses snort. Black Kettle, with care, ties a white cloth to his staff. He then raises his staff in the air—a flag of truce, a symbol of surrender, the same gesture he had once made at Sand Creek. He raises it high, facing the far bank where the shapes of soldiers now begin to emerge.

The cavalry halts on the opposite side of the river. No words are spoken. Only the wind speaks now, howling across the landscape. A lone wolf cries out in the distance, its wail echoing across the frozen plain like a premonition. Then, two shots ring out—sharp, brutal, and echoing. The images slow. The animation lingers as the bullets find their targets. The bodies of Chief Black Kettle and the medicine woman fall into the snow. There is no charge. No shouts. No warning. Only the abrupt, heartless punctuation of death.

The screen fades from the fall to the aftermath. Their lifeless forms lie twisted in the snow. Blood seeps into the frozen earth, red against white. Their faces are calm. The staff with the white flag is shown on the ground beside them, now a cruel symbol of misplaced faith.

This sequence does not need dialogue; it speaks volumes in silence. The artistry of the animation does not obscure the horror; rather, it elevates it. Every frame is deliberate. Every movement restrained. The snow, the stillness, the solitary howl—all of it tells the story of betrayal, of genocide, of a people who tried to make peace and were met with steel and fire.

This reenactment is not fictionalized drama—it is a visual truth; a memorial set to motion. Chief Black Kettle was not a warrior in this moment—he was a diplomat, a man seeking refuge, safety, survival. And yet, this scene reveals the cold reality that to surrender to white power was not to be spared, but to be destroyed.

By presenting this atrocity through animation, Peck invites the viewer to feel the weight of this moment not just intellectually, but emotionally. The medium strips away the desensitizing gloss of conventional war documentaries and demands attention. This was not war—it was murder.

The imagery remains etched: the blowing snow, the silent river, the lifeless bodies, the white flag on the ground between them. A truce offered. A truce denied. A people betrayed again.

"The Past Has a Future We Never Expect."

The screen fades in, pulling the viewer back into the humid, lush wilderness of Africa. A new scene begins—but it is also a return. The camera pans across dense, green foliage, alive with the low hum of insects and distant bird calls. The light is muted beneath the jungle canopy.

We find the Black clergyman, as a reminder, this is provided for whites viewing the documentary in order to flip the script, so that they may see the story from our lens. The clergyman is now seated on a stump, where earlier he had knelt in prayer. His posture is still, his shoulders slightly slumped, his face marked by a quiet sorrow that now refuses to be hidden. He holds his letter in his hand—the letter he had written to his beloved. In the prior scene, we had watched him writing it, hopeful, joyful, carefully choosing his words, recounting the wonder of his journey and expressing longing to see her again. Now he is shown destroying the letter in the fire he made. His conscious is clearly disturbed by his own betrayal of justice.

Earlier in the film, this clergyman had committed a brief but brutal act—he had kicked a white enslaved child who had already been beaten severely. The scene offered no justification, no explanation—only the jarring reality that the victim was a child, and the perpetrator, a man of faith. It was not retribution. The child had done nothing. It was an impulsive act of cruelty—a moment in which the clergyman himself became complicit in the very dehumanization that had scarred generations before him.

And now, sitting alone in the African wilderness, he is haunted by that act. The letter in his hand no longer speaks truth. It was cheerful. It was full of hope. But now it feels dishonest. It does not reflect the man he has discovered himself to be. He is now facing a small fire nearby—embers glowing, feeding on the fallen brush of the forest. Without ceremony, he places the letter into the flames. The parchment catches, curls, darkens. The ink turns to smoke.

As the camera lingers on this quiet, devastating moment, Raoul Peck is providing narration, his voice low and pensive. He is quoting from an unnamed—perhaps a scholar, perhaps a survivor, perhaps a witness to human evil—but his words echo with unsettling resonance. "Some things are so evil that it is enough that they simply happen. They don't need to be given a second existence by being retold."

The camera shows the clergyman's face—still, heavy with conviction. There is no weeping, no dramatic gesture—only silence. His silence says everything. Peck continues, still quoting the unknown voice: "That's what I think, on some days anyway," "Other days I think the opposite." "The past has a future we never expect."

There is no conclusion to this scene—no judgment rendered, no redemption offered. Only the haunting truth of complicity. That even a preacher can lose sight of grace. That guilt, when it awakens, leaves a man with nothing but silence—and a burning letter that will never be read.

CHAPTER 10

The Living and the Dying: We Don't Want to Remember

A new sequence begins. Black-and-white video footage rolls across the screen—aged, silent images of a steamboat gliding slowly down a broad African river. While on the bank, the simple beauty of village life, thatched huts rest under the weight of time, as Native Africans move about, tending to their livestock, children playing nearby. These Indigenous People look on in curiosity while the rhythm of life, once undisturbed, flows with the current of the river.

Then, in stark white letters, a phrase appears across the screen: "We do not want to remember." The steamboat continues to drift forward, cutting through the heart of the continent. The camera lingers on villagers who glance toward the vessel—some curiously, others expressionless, as though already accustomed to the unfamiliar presence of outsiders.

New words now fade into view across the screen: "Laws are made to bind the weak, to be broken by the strong." The screen then reads: "Colonial Exhibition Entrance – France, 1924." The next image is a still photograph of a walled enclosure to an exhibit. Appearing on the grand archway of the structure, where entrance was permitted: "Village Africain." Such exhibitions revealed a grotesque display, a human zoo of sorts—Indigenous Peoples transported and exhibited before white onlookers like curiosities in a museum.

Also appearing on the screen, as Raoul provides commentary, are the following: Colonial Exhibition, Germany, 1907; Coney Island, New York, USA; Orleans, France, 1905; Colonial Exhibition, Paris, France, 1905; Colonial Exhibition, Paris, 1905.

Raoul, continuing with his narration, says: One of the fundamental ideas of the 19th century was that there are races, peoples, nations, and tribes that are in the process of dying out. Or as Prime Minister of England, Lord Salisbury, expressed it in his famous speech in Albert Hall on May 4th, 1898, "One can roughly divide the nations of the world into the living and the dying. The weak nations become increasingly weaker, and the strong, stronger."

As the narration continues, images cycle through of colonized peoples across continents—Africa, Asia, Oceania, and the Americas. Black-and-white portraits of Native men and women, some forced into European attire, postured before the camera. Others still are surrounded by missionaries, soldiers, or traders—those so-called agents of "civilization."

Raoul continues: "It was in the nature of things, he said, that the living nations would fraudulently encroach on the territory of the dying." He spoke the truth. During the 19th century, Raoul explains, "Europeans had encroached on vast territories around the world. The word genocide had not yet been invented, but the matter existed."

Peck adds, "Joseph Conrad may not have heard Lord Salisbury's speech. He had no need to. Conrad could no more avoid hearing of the ceaseless genocide that marked his century than any of his contemporaries could. It is we who have suppressed it."

Raoul's voice lowers: *"We do not want to remember."*

A new scene appears on the screen. Vast columns of uniformed Nazi soldiers are shown, colorful footage capturing them as they march in strict formation or stand in chilling stillness. It is a display of overwhelming, methodical force, eerily silent, save for the solemn score playing underneath. As this image lingers, Raoul Peck's voice enters: "We do not want to remember."

The screen fades into another historical moment—Queen Victoria's Diamond Jubilee Procession, London, 1897. Ornate carriages pass through cheering crowds, British troops from every corner of the empire proudly marching in military regalia. Colonial subjects—Indians, Africans, and Asians in colorful uniforms or traditional dress—are paraded like trophies before the throne of empire.

Peck's narration cuts in again as he completes his thought: "We would prefer for genocide to have begun and ended with Nazism. This would indeed be most comforting."

The camera pans across scenes of celebration and opulence in London. But the jubilation is laced with something darker—a deep irony. Raoul continues: "For sure, the nine-year-old Adolf Hitler was not in Albert Hall either when Lord Salisbury was speaking. He had no need to. He knew it already."

The film begins to overlay these imperial festivities with a deeper subtext. The musical theme continues. The pomp of empire begins to fade into an unsettling realization. Peck goes on: "The air Hitler and all other Western people in his childhood breathed was soaked in a conviction that imperialism is a biological necessary process which, according to the laws of nature, leads to the inevitable destruction of the 'so-called' lower races."

Still images from colonial exploits begin to flash: Africans and Indians overseen by British officers, Indigenous Australians who had been "civilized" by force. Peck states: "It was a conviction that had already cost millions of lives before Hitler provided his highly personal application."

Then, the screen freezes on a black and white photo—seven German soldiers, posed, rigid and proud. Raoul adds, "But in the mid-19th century, the Germans had still not exterminated any people. So they were able to look more critically on the phenomenon than other Europeans did."

The screen shifts again. A map of Southwest Africa (modern-day Namibia) appears, tracing the lines of German imperial control. "In Southwest Africa in 1904, the Germans demonstrated that they too could master an art that Americans, British, and other Europeans had exercised all through the 19th century: the art of hastening the extermination of a people of inferior culture."

Peck continues: "Following the North American example, the Herero people were banished to reservations, and their grazing lands were handed over to German immigrants and colonial companies."

As Raoul's words ring out, the next image appears—grainy and haunting. A group of European men, rifles in hand, stand proudly over the lifeless bodies of black men, laid out in a dry field like broken statues. Across the screen appears the caption: "Murdered Construction Workers – OMEG Railway Company, 1904."

A photograph of two African men is now shown, presumably, one being a picture of Samuel Maherero. Raoul's voice cuts through the silence once more: "For over two decades, their leader, Samuel Maherero, had signed one treaty after another with the Germans and ceded large areas of land to avoid war." This history and image linger on treaty signings—ink on paper that would never be honored.

Peck continues: "But just as the Americans did not feel bound by their treaties with the Indians, the Germans did not think that, as a higher race, they had any need to abide by treaties they made with the Natives. As in North America, the Germans' plans for immigration presupposed that the Natives were to be relieved of all land of any value." Peck adds: When the Hereros resisted, General Adolf Lebrecht von Trotha ordered their extermination."

Peck's voice sharpens: "Every Herero found within the German borders, with or without weapons, was to be shot." A picture of an old military decree appears in German, with words like "Schießbefehl"—"shooting order"—highlighted. Peck: "But most of them died without direct violence. The Germans simply drove them into the desert and sealed off the border. One didn't yet talk the final solution, but that was what one had in mind."

Peck: In the official account of the war, the German officers wrote: "The army earned the gratitude of the whole Fatherland. The sentence had been carried out, and the Hereros had ceased to be an independent people."

A black and white image is shown of Africans, famished, with emancipated bodies. The scene shifts to a vast, dry desert. The voice of Peck returns. He narrates that 80,000 human beings, Africans, died in the desert. The few thousand that remained were sentenced to hard labor in concentration camps—a new form of incarceration, invented in 1896 by the Spaniards in Cuba.

Now appearing on the screen is the wording: Campo de Concentracion and its English translation, Concentration Camp. The narration continues. "German and English languages, along with their systems of governance, were now forced upon the people and the land."

Peck goes on: Paul Rohrbach wrote in his 1912 bestseller, German Thought in the World, quote, "Existence, be they of peoples or individuals who do not produce anything of value, cannot make any claim to the right to exist."

The next image shown is of Africans in chains, a haunting reminder of their forced subjugation. Another image emerges—two white women appear, educators, pointing toward a poster. The poster presents European scientists and teachers. A caption explains that it is propaganda from the Nazi press, credited to Liselotte Orgel-Köhne.

Then Margaret Sanger is shown addressing an audience. She says, "We believe that married people who have transmissible diseases should not have children." Appearing on the screen is the identification: Margaret Sanger, President of the International Planned Parenthood Federation. Sanger continues: "No couple who has the disease of feeble-mindedness or insanity or epilepsy should have children."

Now, images flash across the screen—idealized white families, clean, composed, well-dressed men and women. Then a large building appears on screen. Printed across its front in large, bold letters: Eugenics and Health Exhibit – American Eugenics Society. Posters line the outside, filled with slogans and charts promising a science that will purify and perfect society.

Peck returns in voiceover: "The over-infatuation with genetic purity, an impressive amount of energy put into the classification of people, a pathological obsession for the concept of race that scientifically does not exist."

As he narrates, black and white photos of guinea pigs appear, used to illustrate how pseudo-science tried to distinguish so-called superior from inferior races. The image displayed that two white guinea pigs, when mated, produce white guinea pigs. And when two black guinea pigs mated, their litter was black. However, when a black and white guinea pig was mated, their litter was called "Hybrid Black."

Then another sign appears on the screen: "These little pigs each have one white and one black determiner." Beneath that reads another chilling phrase: "Some people are born to be a burden on the rest." As these words remain on the screen, video images follow—Indigenous People of color, presented as evidence in this ideology's hierarchy of worth.

A video image now shows an African woman holding her infant child. A white male is shown standing beside the woman. Peck states: "Despite the careful staging, one gesture, an unexpected gesture of irritation not foreseen by the director of this strange display, will betray the masquerade and restore dignity." The video footage then shows the European male patting and touching the head of an African woman. She immediately rejects his touch. She will not have it. Her reaction is not scripted; it is defiance. *It was righteous indignation!*

Now appearing on the screen is the vastness of the beautiful ocean, wide and glistening under the light of day. Imposed on the screen are the words: Sandaga, Senegal. A man of African descent is seen standing on the banks, patiently fishing, his silhouette still against the rhythmic waves.

Additional footage follows—a community of African men preparing to go out to fish. Children are seen playing in the water, carefree, laughing, and splashing. Their joy paints a vivid contrast to the unspoken weight hovering over the scene.

The camera shifts. Another video shows an African man jogging down the road. Behind him, cows wander across the road, a natural coexistence of life in motion. Raoul Peck's narration resumes: "One thing for sure—their way of life is threatened."

A pause… footage now displays an image of an African man, then an African woman, and lastly an African community joined together. Peck then asks, "Has he indeed any right to exist?" "Does she? Do they?" Then, various video images of Africans and other ethnicities are carefully provided one after another, showing their humanity, bearing witness that they are all created in the image of God.

As these images unfold, Nina Simone's song "Feeling Good" is sung in the background.

This final sequence in Part Three does not stand apart; it brings the preceding weight of history into quiet, living focus. After we have witnessed images of colonization, genocide, racial pseudoscience, concentration camps, eugenics, and the dehumanization of African and Indigenous peoples, we are brought face-to-face with what is at stake: Human lives. Real lives. Present lives.

The vast ocean and the calm routines of African fishermen are not just picturesque—they are declarations of survival. The children playing in the water are not simply a visual pause; they are a quiet rebellion against erasure. The man jogging with the cattle shown in the background is not an incidental figure—he is a symbol of continuity. These are lives still being lived, traditions still being upheld, dignity still being preserved.

Raoul Peck's narration cuts through with simple but devastating clarity: "One thing for sure… their way of life is threatened." "Has he indeed any right to exist? Does she? Do they?"

These questions don't exist in a vacuum. They are shaped by everything we have just seen: the theories of racial inferiority that justified genocide; the images of chains, of manipulation through science and staged propaganda; Margaret Sanger's words; the obsession with purity and hierarchy.

These were not abstract ideas; they were campaigns of erasure! They questioned who deserves to live, to thrive, to belong. Raoul asks the question, "After all we now know… indeed, who is to judge?" It is not rhetorical. It is indictment. It is lament. It is resistance.

And then Nina Simone's "Feeling Good" rises—not as a triumphant anthem, but as a counterpoint to all we've seen. In the face of history's atrocities, the presence of joy, of breath, of Black and brown life, becomes its own quiet protest. An image of a baby—so fragile, so full of possibility—anchors this final thought: the future is not abstract either. It is personal. It is born every day, into a world still wrestling with the sins of its past.

This closing ties it all together—not with resolution, but with witness. It tells us that beyond theory and archives, lives continue. And they matter.

CHAPTER 11

"The Bright Colors of Fascism"

The intro into Part 4 of Raoul Peck's documentary is sharp, satirical, and strikingly effective. Through a hypothetical and biting illustration, Peck exposes the absurdity of colonial conquest as a matter of claimed entitlement. He introduces the story of a man who walks into a bar—"My name is Christopher Columbus," the man says. "This bar from now on will be called Hispaniola Lounge." The bar's Black patrons remain silent, but the barman shakes his head and utters dryly, "white people."

It's humorous, but not for the sake of comedy. This moment is layered—it deconstructs centuries of colonial narratives that celebrated so-called "discovery" without ever questioning its legitimacy. What Peck is really doing is bringing the viewer face-to-face with the theft and erasure that underpinned Europe's expansionist conquests. The land was not uninhabited. It was not lost. It was lived on, named, cultivated, defended, and then violently claimed by those who simply declared ownership.

The documentary shifts next into a brief montage showing white people living unbothered, gleeful, and immersed in leisure—dancing in halls, enjoying nature, savoring life. These scenes aren't simply about pleasure—they represent the spoils of systemic privilege. These lives are uninterrupted, free from the traumas depicted in earlier segments—colonial brutality, slavery, racial violence, and scientific dehumanization.

In contrast, this footage is a mirror reflecting the insulation that whiteness has historically provided in colonial and post-colonial societies—an inherited bubble of security, mobility, and access. It's what W.E.B. Du Bois once described as "the wages of whiteness"—the psychological and material benefits conferred upon white people, even the working class, simply for being white.

Peck doesn't let this pass unnoticed. As the film transitions to the 1936 Summer Olympics in Berlin, the montage of carefree white joy abruptly gives way to fascism in full spectacle. A lone Olympic torchbearer runs triumphantly, while massive Nazi banners flap in the wind. Adolf Hitler watches, applauds, and grins. The staging of the Olympics, a global symbol of peace and unity, becomes instead a chilling performance of nationalist supremacy.

This was no accident. The 1936 Olympics were a calculated propaganda move by the Nazi regime, designed to showcase a rejuvenated, disciplined, and ideologically unified Germany. Hitler's presence, the omnipresent swastikas, and the orchestrated spectacle were all crafted to present fascism in attractive packaging. The world was invited to marvel at Germany's might and aesthetic precision, while the regime's genocidal ideology was already well in motion behind the scenes.

And so, as the scene transitions, the words appear: Part 4 – "The Bright Colors of Fascism." Peck invites us to consider not just the brutality of fascism, but the seduction of it—how beauty, spectacle, order, and national pride can mask the machinery of hate. The "bright colors" refer to more than literal banners and Olympic pageantry—they speak to the allure of authoritarianism when it cloaks itself in art, culture, and modernity.

This section, then, is not a detour. It is a continuation. The same racial hierarchies that justified the theft of land and the building of empires also undergird the fascist imagination. White supremacy, cloaked in civility or culture, remains central—whether through the myth of the heroic explorer or the staged glory of Hitler's Olympic Games. What's at stake, Peck reminds us, is not just history; it's how that history repeats itself when we refuse to confront it.

Land With People: The Myth of Pristine Wilderness

Raoul says, "Land with no people does not exist. The idea that America was virgin land, a wilderness inhabited by non-people called savages, is a myth. Only through killing and displacement does it become uninhibited."

Before the first British settlements took root, the land that would later be called "North America" was a network of thriving civilizations—Cherokee, Creek, Seminole, Choctaw, Shawnee, and countless others—each with their own systems of governance, agriculture, and trade. The myth of "virgin land" provided the moral cover for one of the most aggressive campaigns of dispossession in human history.

Between 1814 and 1824, during the height of U.S. territorial expansion, land between what is now Kentucky and Florida was seized and transformed into settler territories. This decade marked the culmination of Andrew Jackson's military campaigns against both Native nations and African-descended Maroons who had found refuge among them. The Creek War (1813–1814), which ended with the Treaty of Fort Jackson, ceded over 21 million acres of Creek land to the U.S. government, opening the Southeast to white settlement.

Florida, then under Spanish control, became another target. The First Seminole War (1817–1818), led again by Jackson, was not only about removing Native Seminoles but also about capturing or killing runaway enslaved Africans who had formed Maroon communities within Seminole society. By 1821, the Adams-Onís Treaty transferred Florida from Spain to the United States, cementing white settler control and setting the stage for the forced removal policies that would come to define the century.

This period also overlapped with the so-called "Kentucky frontier," where white migration into Shawnee and Cherokee land intensified. Through treaties often signed under coercion or outright fabricated, Native Nations were pushed further west, and entire communities were erased from their ancestral homes.

By the time the Indian Removal Act was signed in 1830, the blueprint for settler colonialism was fully in motion: declare land "empty," erase its people through warfare, disease, and forced migration, and replace them with white settlers who would inherit the spoils.

Part 4 of the documentary opens under this weight—the myth of emptiness confronted by the reality of blood and displacement that made America's expansion possible.

The footage now transitions into a deeply revealing montage of black and white photographs that emerge one after another, each capturing Native

Americans standing alongside white settlers, soldiers, or government agents. These are not candid moments, but staged images—public relations artifacts meant to portray peace, cooperation, and civility. Yet beneath the stillness of each photo lies the violence of what had just occurred. These pictures are not records of mutual respect—they are records of survival, of conquest, and of forced accommodation. Superimposed over one image appears the title: "Photo Call at Pine Ridge Indian Reservation, South Dakota, 1891."

This date is no coincidence. It comes just one year after the massacre at Wounded Knee, where hundreds of Lakota men, women, and children were slaughtered by U.S. troops. So while the camera shows us posed portraits and manufactured smiles, the soil beneath their feet is still soaked with blood. The very idea of a "photo call" after such atrocity underscores how image-making was weaponized as a tool of erasure—conquest could be sanitized, brutality made palatable, even picturesque.

The film then moves from photographs to museum exhibits—mock Native American villages, reconstructed dwellings, and life-sized statues behind glass. Visitors, mostly white, stroll through these exhibits absorbing a version of history that is static, depersonalized, and curated for entertainment. Native Peoples, once sovereign nations, have now been reduced to spectacle. This transformation—from living cultures to anthropological artifacts—is itself a form of violence. It freezes Indigenous identity in a pre-modern past, suggesting that Native Americans no longer exist as contemporary political or cultural agents. They are trapped in dioramas, displayed as remnants.

Over these images, Raoul Peck's voice returns. He intimates that the bid for independence by the United States—a revolution supposedly rooted in the ideas of liberty, democracy, and equality—was never truly compatible with its founding reality: the supremacy of one race over all others, the exploitation of land and labor, the obliteration of Indigenous life. This contradiction—between lofty ideals and brutal practices—demanded reconciliation. But instead of confronting the truth, a myth was born.

To resolve this tension, a new national identity was constructed: not a biologically mixed race, but an imagined cultural synthesis. Peck describes this invention as "the birth of the U.S. American race"—a symbolic merging of the Native and the European. But as he makes clear, this was never intended to be an actual union. "God forbid," he says ironically, "not a biological merger." Rather, it was a narrative—a fantasy—crafted to imply that Native identity had been absorbed, neutralized, and ultimately dissolved into something superior and white.

This process excluded both Native Americans and African Americans. Their presence was permitted only as foils—as backdrops, as cautionary tales, or as noble savages and faithful servants used to define what white America was not. They could participate only by being othered.

The screen then displays hand-drawn illustrations of the mythic American frontiersman—stoic, rugged, and white. Here, Raoul Peck quotes D. H. Lawrence, reflecting on the character of James Fenimore Cooper's Deerslayer. Lawrence writes: "All the other stuff—the love, democracy, the floundering into lust—is a sort of by-play. The essential American soul is hard, isolate, stoic, and a killer. It has never yet melted."

Peck wields this quote not as a poetic flourish, but as a piercing diagnosis. In Lawrence's words, we find the brutal self-understanding of the

American myth: that beneath the talk of equality and freedom lies a deeper, more enduring identity—an identity forged in conquest, hardened by isolation, and sustained by violence.

This segment of the documentary extends the narrative already established in earlier scenes. Just as the United States crafted an external image of democratic righteousness while practicing settler colonialism, here we see how it simultaneously constructed an internal identity—one that justified domination by mythologizing itself. It wasn't enough to erase Indigenous and Black existence through war and policy; their cultural and historical memory had to be overwritten.

The myth of the essential white American—self-made, self-reliant, and above all, innocent—is what allowed the U.S. to claim moral high ground while standing on stolen land and profiting from stolen labor. Peck's critique is unflinching: America is not just a nation of immigrants or ideals—it is a nation of curated images, selective memory, and foundational lies.

Through these layered visuals and quotations, Peck exposes the machinery behind American identity formation—how violence becomes invisible, and how myth becomes national truth.

Osama bin Laden: "Geronimo"

This portion of the documentary marks a jarring but deliberate shift—from the distant past of settler colonialism to the sharp edge of America's modern military machine. Yet despite the shift in time and setting, the underlying theme remains the same: the continuity of imperial power, myth-making, and racial coding within the American project. The video transitions from photographs and dioramas to the cinematic realism of modern warfare.

The screen fills with the haunting imagery of a Black Hawk helicopter—its dark silhouette descending against a dusty desert landscape in Pakistan. The footage, though animated, mirrors real events with unsettling precision. Navy SEAL Soldiers leap from the aircraft, rifles drawn, as the camera follows them breaching the high walls of a compound. The mood is tense, surgical, and glorified.

Inside a sterile situation room, President Barack Obama, Secretary of State Hillary Clinton, and other top officials sit before a live feed, watching every moment unfold. Their faces are fixed with a combination of resolve and apprehension. The voice of Raoul Peck resumes, narrating with careful detachment: this is the May 2, 2011, Navy SEAL operation that resulted in the assassination of Osama bin Laden.

The spectacle of war, once waged with muskets on horseback against Native warriors, is now executed with night-vision goggles and drone surveillance. But the logics of conquest and domination remain eerily familiar. And then comes the line that cuts through the patriotic narrative: "Geronimo." That was the code name reportedly assigned to Osama bin Laden by U.S. military intelligence.

The New York Daily News noted the secrecy surrounding that designation—how the reasons for using it remained one of the "biggest mysteries" of the Black Ops mission. But as Peck states plainly, it was no mystery at all—not to the Navy SEALs who executed the mission, not to the American officials watching from the safety of Washington, and certainly not to any Native American who heard it. To them, the insult was unmistakable.

As the narration continues, archival images of Geronimo appear on screen—his face stern and determined, a symbol of resistance. Born Goyaałé or Goyathlay, meaning "the one who yawns," Geronimo was a legendary Apache leader who resisted Mexican and American incursions into Indigenous lands. He was not a terrorist, but a freedom fighter—one of the fiercest adversaries the U.S. military encountered during its brutal expansion westward.

For Native peoples, Geronimo represents resilience and dignity in the face of genocide. To code bin Laden with Geronimo's name is not just a racial slight; it is an act of historical violence—a continuation of how the United States defines its enemies, recasts its heroes, and manipulates its symbols.

This moment in the documentary functions as a damning juxtaposition. On the one hand, America hails its technological precision, its global reach, its ability to strike fear into its enemies. On the other hand, it continues to carry the same colonial mindset that casts Indigenous resistance as savagery and Indigenous leaders as enemies of civilization. To code an anti-colonial Apache warrior as a foreign terrorist is to collapse time and geography, conflating all non-Western resistance into a single enemy.

Peck does not need to raise his voice; the images and associations speak for themselves. This isn't just about one military operation or one historical figure. It's about the persistence of a worldview where America is the righteous actor and all others—whether Indigenous peoples defending their homeland or Muslim militants reacting to U.S. interventions—are defined solely in opposition to American power. The myth of American innocence requires that resistance always be labeled as aggression, that heroes of colonized people be rendered villains in the empire's story.

Thus, this scene ties seamlessly to everything that has preceded it. The legacy of conquest, the rebranding of genocide as destiny, the use of visual culture to shape national memory—all of it now arrives in the present moment. Peck shows us that American imperialism didn't end with the closing of the frontier. It simply put on a new uniform, flew different flags, and kept marching.

Words Matter: Linguistic Psychology

This segment of the documentary intensifies its critique of American militarism by exposing the linguistic and psychological continuity between settler colonialism and modern warfare. As U.S. military tanks are shown rumbling across desert sands—presumably in Iraq or Afghanistan—Raoul Peck's voice overlays the footage with an unsettling truth: the past is never truly past. It simply finds new terrain, new names, new enemies, and new justifications.

The code word "Geronimo," used to identify Osama bin Laden, is not an anomaly. Nor is it isolated military slang. It is part of a larger pattern, one deeply embedded in the language, training, and worldview of the American war machine.

Peck points out how the term "Indian Country" is used in military parlance to describe hostile zones or areas behind enemy lines. This is not a casual phrase; it is systemic. It reflects a deeply rooted metaphor in which modern U.S. enemies are cast in the same symbolic role as the Native Americans once targeted for extermination.

The viewer is left to reckon with the reality that American imperial identity was forged not just through war abroad but through the annihilation of Indigenous nations at home. The use of this term serves to remind soldiers and commanders alike that the U.S. military still sees itself reenacting the Indian Wars—a perpetual mission of domination against any people labeled as "other."

Images flash across the screen: Black Hawk helicopters, Apache gunships, Tomahawk missiles—all military equipment named after Native American figures or tribes. This naming is not homage. It is appropriation turned weaponization. These names are stripped of their cultural and spiritual significance and rebranded as tools of war. As Peck coldly narrates, "All U.S. wars reenact fundamentally the Indian wars." That is, the template for American violence abroad was established long before Vietnam, Iraq, or Afghanistan—in the scorched earth of the plains, in the Trail of Tears, in the burned-out villages of Wounded Knee and Sand Creek.

As the screen transitions to historical imagery of Indigenous Americans, a painting of colonial warriors is then shown holding high a Native head impaled on a spear—the connection between symbolic and physical violence becomes undeniable.

Peck draws on military historian John Grenier, who wrote extensively about America's first military tradition: not heroic defense or tactical brilliance, but genocidal violence against Indigenous peoples. Grenier argues that the foundational American military identity was forged in the extermination of Native communities and that this brutal tradition has been passed down—unacknowledged but deeply embedded—through each generation of American warfare.

Raoul Peck drives the point home with chilling clarity: "The chief characteristic of irregular war is extreme violence against civilians." And that is exactly what shaped U.S. military policy—from the frontier wars to Fallujah. "Kill anything that moves, take no prisoners"—a phrase used in Vietnam, but one that echoes with familiarity across centuries of American conflict. Such language reduces the enemy to subhuman status, rationalizing annihilation as strategy, murder as policy.

Hunting "Indians" for Pay

And then comes perhaps the most damning revelation: in California, the extermination of Native Americans was not only legal—it was subsidized. In the mid-1800s, it was state policy to reward settlers for hunting Indigenous people. "Five dollars for a head." "Fifty cents for a scalp." In 1854, the U.S. federal government paid out over $1 million to Indian hunters—a grotesque economy of death. As the screen displays a historical notice as listed in The Daily Republican, proclaimed, "The state reward for dead Indians has been increased to $200," the viewer confronts a hard truth: American capitalism and expansion were lubricated with blood.

This moment in the documentary strips away the illusions of moral superiority and national innocence. It forces the audience to reckon with the fact that U.S. military tradition was not born in the defense of liberty, but in the systemic slaughter of those who stood in the way of expansion—first Native Americans, and later anyone abroad who dared resist U.S. dominance. Peck reveals that this is not a deviation from American values; this is the tradition.

The rhetoric of democracy and freedom has always been accompanied by the machinery of death and dispossession. The genius of this segment lies in its unflinching juxtaposition: modern tanks in the Middle East beside 19th-century bounties for Indigenous heads; military jargon beside historical genocide; sanitized official narratives beside the raw, bloody truth. Peck's method is not to shout but to unveil, layer by layer, how the past has been institutionalized, repackaged, and operationalized in the name of American greatness.

The result is a sobering indictment: American warfare, past and present, is less about liberation than it is about maintaining a violent global and domestic order shaped by racial supremacy and settler conquest.

CHAPTER 12

The Second Amendment and "The Cult of the Gun"

The documentary shifts seamlessly from the historical landscape of sanctioned state violence abroad to the deeply entrenched culture of armed resistance at home. As images flash of heavily armed American civilians—often white men in tactical gear, wielding military-grade weapons—Raoul Peck's narration connects them to a long lineage of settler militancy. These are not random enthusiasts or fringe radicals. They are the ideological and biological descendants of those who once cleared the frontier, enforced racial hierarchies, and clung to the myth of divine American exceptionalism.

The camera pans across these contemporary militia-style groups, many of whom are vocal defenders of the Second Amendment. But Peck immediately reframes their claim to patriotic self-defense. "They assert that they represent "the people"—a phrase historically coded to exclude the enslaved, the Indigenous, the immigrant, and the poor.

Their interpretation of the Second Amendment is not merely about individual liberty or personal protection. It's about maintaining a racialized vision of government ordained by what they believe is a God-given covenant. The Constitution, in their eyes, is not a "living document" but a sacred script—one whose origin story is mythologized and whose exclusions are conveniently ignored.

As Raoul speaks, the Second Amendment appears on screen, but it is not reverenced—it is interrogated. His narration cuts deeper: "and to control enslaved Africans." This single clause shatters the dominant narrative. The right to bear arms was never neutral. From the very beginning, American gun culture was intertwined with the need to suppress slave revolts, patrol plantations, and enforce white dominance. The militia system that the founders protected was a slave-holding apparatus. The arms were not only for defense against tyranny but for the subjugation of Black bodies.

Then enters Roxanne Dunbar-Ortiz, a historian who has consistently confronted the uncomfortable truths of American origins. Her voice takes over. As footage shows her addressing students at UCLA in February 2020, she states plainly: "Roughly three-fourths of gun owners are men, and 82% are white." The numbers speak volumes. This is not random. This is demographic concentration. White male gun ownership isn't simply cultural—it's political. Ortiz continues, "Taken together, about 61% of adults who own guns are white men." These statistics reveal a deep connection between identity, history, and firepower.

Her conclusion is clear and inescapable: "We cannot make sense of gun hoarding and the cult of the gun if we don't deal with *white nationalism*. And we can't deal with white nationalism without dealing with United States history." This is the heart of the critique. American gun culture is not an isolated phenomenon—it is a symptom of a deeper legacy: conquest, fear of the "other," racialized power, and the myth of rugged individualism.

The narration returns to Peck, who gently but incisively reflects: "My friend Roxanne told me, as men of their times, the founders created the most perfect document ever written. For the most perfect country on earth." But he doesn't leave the statement there. With piercing honesty, he adds, "But today we can see the warts, and they ruin the picture." What was once glorified as a shining vision of liberty is now exposed, scarred by its exclusions, hypocrisies, and violent origins.

This segment ties in powerfully with the previous sections of the documentary. Just as U.S. foreign wars mirror the brutal logic of the Indian Wars, so too does modern American gun culture mirror the settler logic of domestic control. Whether through drone strikes abroad or open-carry laws at home, the same foundational logic is at play: domination disguised as defense, whiteness masquerading as patriotism, and fear dressed in constitutional language.

By bringing Roxanne Dunbar-Ortiz into the frame, Peck strengthens his argument that the cult of the gun is not just a policy issue or cultural debate—it is a historical echo of settler colonialism and slavery. It is the continuity of a nation unwilling to reckon with the full weight of its origin story.

The documentary then provides a montage—small photographs flickering across the screen like memory fragments—of American citizens, men and women, children and elders, Black and white, Indigenous and immigrant, Latin-x and Asian, Muslim and Jewish, rich and poor, urban and rural. These are not stock images of sanitized patriotism but raw, human snapshots: protests, bus rides, weddings, soldiers, steelworkers, street musicians – everyday people. They are the living contradictions of

America—citizens who have each, in their own way, inherited the promises and the betrayals of the so-called "land of the free."

As these images cascade—one after another, dozens upon dozens—the viewer hears the soulful, aching voice of Sharon Jones and the Dap-Kings singing "This Land is Your Land." Woody Guthrie's classic protest anthem, often misremembered as a feel-good folk tune, is here reclaimed in its radical form. It does not affirm national pride; it interrogates it.

The lyrics, stripped of their patriotic sugarcoating and sung by a Black woman whose own ancestors may have tilled American soil without recompense, now accompany images of a multiracial America still grappling with the question of who truly belongs. The song is no longer a celebration—it becomes a lamentation and a demand.

Assault Against So-Called American Exceptionalism

The camera then cuts to a new image: birds soaring freely through the sky. At first, they appear to symbolize hope or transcendence, but as the next words are spoken, this image becomes ironic. Over the wings of the birds, Raul Peck's voice cuts in: "Make America Great Again," he said. Then, almost immediately, the camera—and the narrative—tightens with a pointed question from Peck: *"When exactly was it great? I mean, really great? And for whom?"*

It is here that the documentary launches a direct assault on the myth of American exceptionalism. The image immediately following this question is not of fireworks, founding fathers, or amber waves of grain—but a vast cotton field, stretching toward the horizon. No longer is greatness symbolized by industry or liberty. Instead, we are brought face-to-face with the true economic engine of the early United States: slavery.

The screen now displays a photograph—African American men laboring, their backs bent, under the weight of cotton or shipyard goods, under the supervision of white men. These are not isolated scenes; they are representative of centuries of racialized labor that underwrote America's rise.

As Peck narrates, he places this moment in historical context: "Around 1831, U.S. cotton made up almost half of the world's production." Cotton was not a regional crop—it was a global commodity. The wealth it generated lined the pockets of Southern plantation owners and Northern industrialists alike. As Peck makes clear, "The elite in the South became extremely wealthy. The elite in the North became extremely wealthy as well…"

The impact was not merely economic—it was epochal. Cotton, produced by enslaved hands, helped spark the Industrial Revolution. In the visual sequence, a placard reading "Cotton Exchange Building" appears on a door, not unlike the unassuming signage one might find on a bank or brokerage. But behind that modest sign was an international network of blood-soaked commerce.

Peck continues his narration: in the early years, "enslaved men and women had to clean cotton with their bare hands," pulling seeds from fiber until their fingers bled. The invention of the cotton gin by Eli Whitney revolutionized this process—but rather than decreasing the demand for enslaved labor, it dramatically increased it. As cotton production soared, so did the need for more labor, more land, and more exploitation. "Cotton also destroyed the soil," says Peck, "so Southerners and Northerners plundered more Indian land, while using slaves' bodies as a commodity, the most lucrative enterprise around."

This is where the documentary drops its most devastating economic truth: slavery wasn't just a backward system propped up by hate. It was a modern enterprise, the most lucrative in its time. "More profitable than all land, banks, railroads, factories, and gold products together," Peck explains. Slaves were not just workers—they were assets. They were used as collateral for mortgages. Bought, sold, insured, and securitized. It was a system where bodies became banking tools—where the commodification of human life formed the basis of American finance.

To drive this point home, Peck tells a story that deflates every myth of Jeffersonian nobility. Thomas Jefferson, author of the Declaration of Independence and champion of liberty, mortgaged 150 of his enslaved workers to build Monticello. The financing came from a Dutch company. America's founding father, whose words declared that "all men are created equal," literally mortgaged Black lives to fund his estate—while Europe silently bankrolled the transaction.

This is not mere historical trivia—it is a moral indictment. "Mortgaging people to buy more people," says Peck, succinctly. It is a phrase that lays bare the madness and method of American capitalism. Even as parts of Europe abolished slavery by 1848, European powers remained economically complicit in American slavery—reaping the profits while distancing themselves from the sin.

Thus, when Peck asks, "When exactly was it great?" The cotton fields and the slave mortgaging, the forced Indian removals, and the silent European investments provide the clearest possible answer: it was great for some, and on the backs of others.

And so the images of smiling citizens from every corner of the globe, shown moments earlier, are now recontextualized. The diversity of modern America exists not because of national benevolence, but because of historical struggle. The people who today call this land their home—Black, brown, Indigenous, immigrant—do so in spite of the foundations of this country, not because of them.

Peck is not merely recounting history; he is dismantling mythology. He is showing that the greatness invoked by slogans like "Make America Great Again" is selective memory—a longing for a past where whiteness ruled unchallenged, and capitalism went unchecked. And to confront that mythology, he insists, we must deal with the whole story: not only the founding fathers, but the fields of cotton; not only the Constitution but the commodification of flesh; not only the American dream but the racialized nightmare that financed it.

In this segment, Peck then completes a crucial movement in his documentary. He transitions from critique to confrontation, from examination to judgment. The birds flying in the sky—once, a symbol of freedom—now seem almost mocking, because true freedom cannot take flight on a foundation built from chains.

The screen shifts to bold lettering: "Responses of Victims," accompanied by the words: Submission · Suicide · Hiding · Escape · Resistance · Assimilation · Demoralization. Raoul Peck's voice overlays these terms: "Raphael Lemkin wrote, 'slavery may be called cultural genocide par excellence. It is the most effective and thorough method of destroying a culture and of de-socializing human beings."

Resistance Through Dance

As these words settle, the air fills with the haunting notes of "A Rapahoe Ghost Dance," song number 73, sourced from James Mooney's late-19th-century recordings. Peck continues: "By 1890, disarmed, held in concentration camps, their children taken away, half-starved, the Lakota and Dakota survivors found a new form of resistance—Ghost dancing."

The screen reads: Pine Ridge Indian Reservation, South Dakota, 1891, then plays actual footage of Native Americans performing the Ghost Dance. A second title appears: "Sioux Ghost Dance, provided by Thomas A. Edison, Incorporated, 1894."

Peck explains, "It was a simple dance performed by everyone in the open, requiring only a specific kind of handmade ribbon skirt in the belief that it might protect the dancers from gunfire. It spread like wildfire in all directions." He continues: Among the movement's sources was Paiute holy man Wovoka (pictured), whose vision in Nevada prophesied Native rebirth, buffalo return, and colonizer disappearance through nonviolent dance.

Peck recounts: "Native pilgrims journeyed long distances to hear Wovoka's message and to receive directions on how to perform the Ghost Dance, which promised to restore the Indigenous world, make the invaders disappear, and bring the dead warriors and buffalo back."

The dancers moved without rest, often collapsing, only to be replaced by others as the circle continued. When the Ghost Dance reached Sioux lands in 1890, officials falsely claimed that Sitting Bull had ordered the dancers at Pine Ridge to perform ceaselessly. In truth, Sitting Bull resided at Standing Rock, had learned the dance, but had not issued any orders. The ceremony was spontaneous.

Why this matters within the documentary's arc:

1. Cultural resistance as survival: After centuries of forced submission, genocide, and assimilation, the Ghost Dance emerged not as escapism, but as a vibrant assertion of cultural identity and hope—spiritual defiance rooted in belief, not arms.

2. Cultural genocide and dehumanization: Lemkin's definition draws a clear line: "slavery and settler colonialism aimed not only at physical annihilation but at erasing entire ways of being." The Ghost Dance directly confronted that erasure.

3. Colonial fear and reaction: What was peaceful prayer became proof of rebellion in the eyes of U.S. agents. Resistance—especially of Indigenous spiritual and cultural forms—was met with brutal repression.

4. Unbroken line of opposition: From African spiritual traditions under slavery to Native resistance movements, oppressed peoples have forged counter-visions of liberation. The Ghost Dance is among the most potent of these—driven by faith, fearlessness, and refusal.

This section reconnects with the broader documentary themes:

- The repeated patterns of domination—from slaughter to enforced silence—left room for new forms of resistance.

- Genocide and dispossession did not extinguish Indigenous consciousness. Instead, it forced the Indigenous peoples to adapt, to move toward spiritual and communal renewal.

- Ultimately, Lémkin's insight and the Ghost Dance's resurgence stand as a testament: cultural destruction can kill societies—but it cannot kill their spirit when defenders refuse to stop dancing.

General Sherman's Heartless Massacre of Native Peoples

The screen now shifts dramatically to a formal gathering—an opulent hall lined with velvet drapes, and the stiff posture of men in uniform. A crowd of journalists presses forward with notepads and flashbulbs. The date appears on screen: January 7, 1891. The location: New York City. Then another title fades in: "A few days after the Battle of Wounded Knee."

A voice cuts through the crowd, "General Sherman! General Sherman!"—the name was called with urgency. Sherman stands at the center of attention, flanked by other high-ranking military men in full uniform. One journalist shouts, "How do you see the end of this revolt?" Another interrupts, "Are there civilian casualties?" Then, cutting straight to the point: "How many savages have you killed?"

General William Tecumseh Sherman, without pause, smirks and replies, "Lots of familiar faces." The room erupts in laughter—an unsettling chuckle echoing the grotesque casualness with which Indigenous life was discarded.

Another reporter poses a question with mock admiration: "General, how do you keep such vigor after such an exhausting battle?" Sherman answers coldly, "Well, riding horses and killing Indians does keep one crisp and fresh." Again, laughter. The mood in the room reflects not remorse, not reflection, but entertainment.

A third journalist presses on: "What lessons do you draw from this campaign? Is there an end to these permanent revolts?" Sherman responds, "Indians must either work or starve. They never have worked, they won't work now, and they never will work." Someone in the crowd attempts a gesture of conscience, asking, "But should not the government supply them with enough to keep them from starvation?" Sherman retorts, "Are you going to pay for it?"

Then the room falls quieter as a more pointed question emerges: "Who shot Sitting Bull?" Sherman shrugs it off: "How is that important? He resisted arrest and was shot." Another voice: "What about Bigfoot?" Sherman responds sharply, "What about him?" The journalist pushes, "It's said that they had him surrounded." Sherman answers dismissively, "Huh. Huh. That's what the *fake press* wants us to believe."

Questions swirl now with greater heat: "What about Custer's regiment? It's said they wanted revenge." Another follows: "And what about the 25 soldiers killed by friendly fire?" Sherman answers flatly, without shame: "Shit happens."

The room murmurs. But Sherman, unmoved, leans forward and asks the gathered press, "Why is it you journalists are always trying to make things more complicated than they are?" He adds coldly, "It was a search action. We told them to surrender and hand over their weapons."

One journalist replies, "Which they did." Sherman responds defiantly as he stares at the audience, "That's your version! Appearing on the screen, Wounded Knee Massacre Est. Indians killed: 300. Survivors: 51 (4 men, 47 women). Army casualties: 25 dead.

Actual gripping and graphic pictures show these murdered Native Americans' bodies lying on the ground where they were massacred! Another haunting picture shows the dead Indigenous people being thrown into a mass grave. Following was a picture showing the dead bodies of Yellow Bird, Medicine Man, Big Foot, chief of the Miniconjou, Lakota Sioux.

This chilling reenactment, involving General Sherman, based on documented accounts and real sentiments expressed by military leadership of the time, is no dramatic embellishment—it captures the contemptuous spirit with which Indigenous life was devalued, dehumanized, and ultimately exterminated under the banners of law, order, and American expansion.

Lying on the snow-covered ground are the broken bodies of the Native People—massacred by General Sherman and his army. Several pictures are displayed on screen, each showing the bodies lying exactly where they were killed. Captions on two of the pictures depict Yellow Bird, the medicine man, and Bigfoot, chief of the Miniconjou Lakota Sioux. Another picture shows a mass grave with human bodies piled one upon another, while other Indigenous bodies lie beside the pit. White soldiers are shown discarding the dead.

The scene then dramatically shifts. The documentary provides an image of the character Dorothy from The Wizard of Oz, directed by Victor Fleming. The film's title appears on the screen. The scene that follows is the one in which Dorothy, a white young lady, has fallen asleep. As the snow begins to fall while she lies on the floor of the beautiful poppy field, she wakes from her sleep. The lion and the scarecrow, major characters in the movie, also awaken with her. The song "Follow the Yellow Brick Road" by Judy Garland is softly heard as Raoul begins his commentary.

He says: "Five days after the sickening events at Wounded Knee, Lyman Frank Baum, a Dakota Territory settler who would become very famous years later for writing The Wonderful Wizard of Oz, wrote to the Aberdeen Saturday Pioneer newspaper: 'The Pioneer has before declared that our only safety depends upon the total extermination of the Indians.'"

While this commentary is being given, a picture of a sign appears on screen. It reads: "The Land of the Dakotas, Aberdeen in 1880." Behind the sign is the picture of a Native child, presumably standing with its father and mother.

Peck continues to quote Baum: "Having wronged them for centuries, we had better, in order to protect our civilization, follow it up by one more wrong and wipe these untamed and untameable creatures from the face of the earth."

The Paradox of Snow

The screen now shows a reservation of Indigenous People huddled or herded together. The message is clear, nor was this not a time event for the Indigenous Peoples. The people who once freely roamed and cultivated this land are now confined, reduced to shadows of their former sovereignty.

And now back to the Wizard of Oz: there lies Dorothy, unconscious, having fallen under the spell of the enchanted poppy field. Snow begins to fall. But this snow does not bring death. This snow is depicted as life-giving. It stirs Dorothy, the lion, and the scarecrow awake—renewed, revived, restored.

And yet, we have just seen real pictures of real snow—where the bodies of Native People lie cold, still, and lifeless. Covered by the same element that in The Wizard of Oz symbolizes rebirth, hope, and prosperity. For the Indigenous, snow has so often come hand in hand with death. With burial. With silence, hence the paradox of snow.

But for Dorothy and her comrades, it is the beginning of something bright—a yellow brick road, a promised land, a fantasy of new life. The same snow, but a vastly different meaning—life for the settler, death for the Native, again the paradox of snow.

The contrast is devastating. This portion of the documentary does not flinch. It does not soften the edges. It shows how fantasy was used to bury reality. How myth was used to whitewash massacre. How a man who called for the extermination of a people would later become the beloved creator of one of the most iconic fairytales in American history.

The documentary leaves the viewer with the weight of that knowledge: that the land we stand on, sing about, and dream through was soaked in blood—then painted over with stories of wonder, witches, and yellow roads… what an oxymoron.

CHAPTER 13

The Real Fight Remains: The Structure of Terror

Raoul continues his commentary. He says, "The fact is, the Native Americans are still here, and this is still their home." An image is shown of Native Americans standing in solidarity, their fists raised high. This visual moment affirms presence, resilience, and enduring identity. Raoul continues: "And despite some real individual accomplishments, the real fight remains the fight for self-determination and restitution. Anything less would not be acceptable."

Now appearing on screen is the image of Louise Erdrich, an acclaimed Native American writer. The screen then shifts to show a Native woman standing in court, her hand raised, taking an oath of truth. The name presented is: Associate Justice Raquel Montoya-Lewis, Washington Supreme Court.

Next, a sequence of faces and titles is shown: Representative Sharice Davids, Kansas. Representative Ruth Buffalo, North Dakota. Representative Heather Keeler, Minnesota. Deb Haaland, Secretary of the Interior. Russell Means, co-founder of the American Indian Movement.

The documentary now plays archival footage of Russell Means as he speaks before the court. His voice is calm but resolute: "The American Indian individual shall have the right to choose his or her citizenship, and the American Indian nations have the right to choose their level of citizenship and autonomy up to absolute independence."

Superimposed on the screen are the words: "The past in the present." Raoul resumes his commentary. He says, "The same observation could be made about slavery. For slavery, here is a ghost. Both the past and a living presence."

Images now shift. Incarcerated Black men are shown working in cotton fields under guard. A scene that could be mistaken for the 1800s—but it is not. It is today. Raoul continues: "And after 400 years, the problem of historical reparation is how to present that ghost. Something that is, and yet is not."

Images follow of Black men being taken into custody by law enforcement. Another series shows rows of incarcerated Black men in modern prison systems. Raoul continues: "The fact that U.S. slavery has both officially ended and yet continues in many complex forms of institutionalized racism makes its representation particularly burdensome." He does not soften the truth. "As long as genocide, slavery, and the exploitation of human bodies do not convert into reparation—whatever the form—there will never be any peace."

Peck then offers a quote from James Baldwin: "There is scarcely any hope for the American dream because people who are denied participation in it by their very presence will wreck it." These words sit heavy against the backdrop of present-day incarceration, echoing the legacy of slavery. Not only a past injustice but an enduring structure.

Superimposed on the screen are the words: Galveston, Texas, August 2019. Peck begins to narrate: "The facts are staring us in the face. Time is not a chronological continuity." He is quoting Haitian scholar Michel-Rolph Trouillot from his book Silencing the Past: "It is the range of disjointed moments, practices, and symbols that thread the historical relations between events and narratives."

As Raoul continues his narration, the screen now shifts to images of Jewish men—Holocaust survivors. Slowly, they roll up their sleeves, exposing the tattoos etched into their arms, symbols of the identification system forced upon them during Hitler's regime. These numbers seared into their flesh stand as permanent reminders of state-sponsored terror.

The screen cuts to various global protests—marches in cities across the world, signs raised, voices lifted, feet pounding pavement in demand for justice. Raoul continues: "No amount of historical debate about any of these events, and no amount of guilt, can serve as a substitute for marching in the streets today. What must be denounced here is not so much the reality of the Native American genocide, or the reality of slavery, or the reality of the Holocaust. What needs to be denounced here are the consequences of these realities in our lives and in our life today."

As Peck continues narration, a familiar figure reappears—the "white man," this symbolic composite representing white colonial violence across time. This is the same man who bathed in the river, the same man who soaked himself in the tub, the same man who coldly shot the Native woman in the head.

Now, in a present-day sequence, this same man is riding a motorcycle through a barren, mountainous, semi-desert region. He does not speak.

He does not look back. He simply rides through dust and time, through conquest and consequence.

He is not a man, but an embodiment. A through-line. A visual thread of dominance, entitlement, and erasure. This character, reappearing again and again throughout the documentary, reveals how the spirit of colonialism and the doctrine of white racial superiority have not been buried—they ride still. Through the roads of history, through the highways of the West, in America and abroad.

Haiti: Death at Home - How Empire Silences

The screen then merges into the image of an old church in Haiti, surrounded by lifeless bodies. This haunting stillness reflects the turbulent political violence that has long plagued the country, often fueled by foreign interference and Cold War-era power struggles. Raoul narrates: "I witnessed death in Haiti. Of unknown people—and of friends. Like Antone Izmery or Guy Mallory. Both slain by CIA-linked military. But not all deaths are violent."

Antoine Izméry was a Haitian businessman and a vocal pro-democracy advocate. His assassination in 1993, just outside a church during a mass commemorating the 1988 St. Jean Bosco massacre, became a symbol of the reign of terror that plagued Haiti under the military junta following the U.S.-backed ousting of President Jean-Bertrand Aristide. Guy Malary, Haiti's Minister of Justice, had been working to reform the corrupt judiciary and implement democratic safeguards when he too was gunned down in 1993. Peck's lament is not only personal—it's political. It is a searing indictment of global complicity and selective mourning, the idea that some deaths are deemed grievable while others are erased.

The Assassination of Prime Minister Patrice Lumumba

The scene transitions to an image, perhaps taken in Berlin: a family of three women and one man, one of the ladies being Raoul's mother. Peck resumes: "I accompanied my mother's passing in a hospital room in Voorhees, New Jersey. She who was the first to tell me about Congo's assassinated Prime Minister Patrice Lumumba. I made a film about him too—and my mother is in it."

Patrice Lumumba, the first democratically elected Prime Minister of the Congo following its independence from Belgium in 1960, was a towering figure of African liberation. But within months of taking office, he was deposed, imprisoned, and brutally executed in a plot aided by Belgian intelligence and the CIA. His death marked one of the Cold War's most blatant sabotages of African self-determination—a crime that still casts a long shadow. Peck's mother, in telling her son about Lumumba, passed down more than memory—she passed down a radical awareness of *how empire silences*.

We move now to Berlin, Germany, where Peck lived for fifteen years and attended film school. He says: "I spent 15 years of my life in a city called Berlin, in Germany. I went to film school there. My entry project was about the prison of Plötzensee—a Nazi torture compound."

Berlin and Auschwitz Death Camps

On the screen appears the ominous façade of the prison, and affixed to its walls, the words: GEDENKSTÄTTE PLÖTZENSEE—a memorial site to those who were executed there. Plötzensee Prison became a central site for the execution of thousands of political prisoners, resistance fighters, and so-called enemies of the Nazi state. Between 1933 and 1945, over 2,500 people were put to death there, often by guillotine or hanging, in a deliberate effort to instill terror and suppress dissent.

Peck continues: "Not one single day when I lived there did I forget that this country, which produced some of humanity's best philosophers, scientists, and artists, also operated one of the most devastating, scientifically run and engineered killing machines." "Berlin. I know these streets by heart. Every day, I walked under these (massive concrete) arches to my classes at the Technical University. The superimposition of time and images."

Time collapses again. We are now at the gates of Auschwitz II-Birkenau, the largest Nazi extermination camp. A chilling visual unfolds—barbed wire fencing stretches across a vast compound. Peck reflects: "Auschwitz. I went there too. I wanted to see it for myself."

The camera pans across discarded suitcases, left behind by Jews who were deported to the camp, many of whom were gassed upon arrival. The camera lingers over thousands of shoes, piled one upon another, each pair a ghostly remnant of a life extinguished. "More than anything else, it was these details which gave me the clearest sense of horror. I have seen these images before." "In Ntarama, Rwanda, in 2003. I took these exact same photos."

Rwandan Genocide

The screen now shifts continents to Rwanda. The name NTARAMA appears on the screen—once a place of worship, now a permanent memorial to horror. In April 1994, during the Rwandan Genocide, thousands of Tutsi civilians sought refuge in this church, believing it would be a sanctuary. But they were trapped, and hundreds were massacred by Hutu militias and government soldiers—often with machetes, grenades, and clubs. The movie, Hotel Rwanda, released in 2005, captures this massacre. This event does not stand alone,

Peck narrates with sorrow and resolve: "A few hundred people had been slaughtered by Hutu militias and government soldiers in a church. A young man told me about what happened. He had been there. And had escaped through a hole. He showed me the hole. Still there. After ten years."

The parallel is haunting. Rwanda in 1994. Auschwitz in the 1940s. Plötzensee in the '30s and '40s. Haiti in the '90s. Congo in 1961. The names change. The continents change. But *the structure of terror—the machinery of erasure, racial domination, and impunity—remains eerily intact.* Peck's journey, personal and political, draws a line through these historical ruptures, showing us that history is not something we look back on. It is something we still inhabit.

Superimposed on the screen: Sometimes in April, Raoul Peck, 2005. Raoul Peck begins to narrate: "I knew I had seen this picture before." Now shown in the documentary are civilians—mainly children—frightened, defenseless, and unsure of their fate as they look up at their captors. This is a dramatization from the Rwandan Genocide of 1994, when over 800,000 people—mostly Tutsi—were slaughtered in a span of just 100 days while the world watched in silence.

In a dramatized reenactment, a Tutsi teenage girl, visible in the frame with tears tracing down her cheeks, turns to her captors and says with quiet defiance, "We are staying together." Her words, though soft, ring with the kind of courage that history records too late.

The camera does not cut away. The soldiers raise their rifles and fire—mercilessly—executing the children and all others who had been captured. It is a moment that bears witness not just to the loss of life, but to the collapse of humanity itself!

Then the voice of Alison Des Forges emerges over the footage—an American historian, human rights investigator, and one of the foremost scholars on Rwanda: "Why didn't the world react? The argument that people didn't know—that's not true. They knew. We know now from intelligence records just how much they knew. That, within hours, they were aware that the killing was being done on an ethnic basis, systematically, that there were lists, that the killers were going through the capital city, choosing out people from certain households and executing them. They knew this."

Her words cut through the haze of denial and international indifference. In the days following the downing of Rwandan President Juvénal Habyarimana's plane, Hutu extremists launched their genocidal campaign. The West, including the United States and the United Nations, had intelligence but chose inaction. The U.N. mission was not only underfunded—it was ordered to scale back during the killings.

Raoul Peck resumes narration: "Alison spent her life documenting the horror. She met world leaders, confronted assassins, engaged doubters, and denounced world institutions hiding behind their silence. She guided me and taught me how to decipher the language of death. And through the monster hiding behind a human mask."

Peck now speaks not of abstractions, but of personal loss. "Alison died in an airplane accident on February 12, 2009, on her way to visit her family in Buffalo. I miss her." The documentary transitions.

Charlottesville, Virginia, and Trump: Flawed Leadership - The Frailty of Power

Now appearing on the screen was Trump Tower, located in Las Vegas. Footage plays of Donald Trump during a press conference held at Trump Tower on August 15, 2017, just days after the violent white supremacist rally in Charlottesville, Virginia. Trump is speaking to reporters about the clashes that took place: "I'm not putting anybody on a moral plane. What I'm saying is this: you had a group on one side, and you had a group on the other. And they came at each other with clubs. And it was vicious, and it was horrible, and it was a horrible thing to watch."

The violence he refers to resulted in the death of Heather Heyer, a 32-year-old counter-protester run down by a car driven into a crowd by a neo-Nazi. The screen now cuts to an aerial view of Trump's estate in Mar-a-Lago, Florida. His voice continues: "I think there's blame on both sides. You look at, you look at both sides. I think there's blame on both sides. I think there's blame on both sides."

The repetition, broadcast live, shocked many—including Republican senators—who expected a condemnation of white supremacy but instead heard an equivalency drawn between fascist mobs and those who resisted them. The next image is of another Trump property: the now-defunct Taj Mahal casino in Atlantic City, a towering monument to excess and financial collapse.

Trump continues: "George Washington was a slave owner. Are we going to take down… are we going to take down the statues? How about Thomas Jefferson? What do you think of Thomas Jefferson? You like him?"

These rhetorical questions came as the nation was reevaluating its memorials to enslavers and Confederates. But rather than reckoning with history, Trump deflected and reframed the conversation as an attack on all American founders—blurring distinctions, shielding systemic racism under the cloak of patriotism.

Then, silently, the screen transitions to an image of Vladimir Putin, followed by a shot of former President George W. Bush and others. Raoul Peck narrates again: "These images project a profound idea of self—or of desperation. Lost souls on a pile of human confusion. The absence of any trace of empathy and genuine humanity is unbearable."

As he speaks, scenes unfold of white European leaders basking in status and comfort—laughing, shaking hands, indulging in their own narrative while the rest of the world faces the fallout of their decisions.

"So deep that we do not recognize it at first. It says who you are. It says what you have become. The stubborn privilege of superiority—and comedy. In times of despair, fear, and insecurity, people are looking for saviors. Any kind will do. But possibly one with easy-sounding solutions that others will pay for. But a complex world calls for complex responses, with at least some minimal aggrievement over the diagnosis. We never listen to the poor. Those who are less poor fear the loss of what they have. And they are rebelling."

Here, Peck names a truth often silenced by power: the rebellion of the insecure, the weaponization of fear, and the self-destruction of privilege. It's the same dynamic that allowed the Rwandan genocide to unfold with machetes in the hands of neighbors. The same dynamic that allows modern demagogues to rise, not because they are persuasive, but because they echo the resentments people are already willing to believe that comes from such flawed leaders.

The Theater of Nationalism: The Hatred of Others

The documentary then cuts to a series of sharp, jolting images: thousands gathered in the streets, fists raised, voices shouting in unison. These are not freedom marches. These are angry demonstrations—xenophobic uprisings—in opposition to immigration. The crowds wave national flags with clenched-jaw pride, many chanting slogans that echo exclusion and racial purity. It is Europe, in the 21st century—but the sentiment is not new.

On the screen appears Marine Le Pen, leader of France's far-right National Rally (formerly National Front), giving a speech to her fervent supporters. Her words, carefully chosen, are laced with the language of "protection," "borders," and "cultural identity"—code for closing the gates to those fleeing wars, poverty, and climate disasters, many of which were either caused or exacerbated by the very powers now refusing them entry.

Immediately following her appearance, the documentary cuts to a historical image: a Nazi rally. Footage of the 1930s fills the screen. The symmetry of banners, the precision of salutes, the sea of flags—all mirroring the contemporary footage that was provided in the documentary. The crowd, then, like the crowd shown, is gripped by the theater of nationalism.

Raoul Peck begins to narrate: "We have been there before—without learning much." It is a devastating indictment, not only of political institutions but of collective memory. "For some reason, we thought that in modern days, fascism would be disguised in bright, friendly colors. So that it would be difficult to recognize. But it is recognizable. The same roar when the leader speaks."

The screen now flashes to footage of Adolf Hitler. He is standing tall, shoulder rigid, surrounded by the people, feeding off their worship. His hand raises into the air, and the crowd responds as if possessed. The Führer's charisma—manipulative, blinding—is matched only by the violence that followed in his wake. The images, though nearly a century old, but not aged with time pulse with urgency.

Raoul continues his narration: "The same hatred of aliens. The same violence. The same projection of wounded manhood. The frailty of power."

Here, Peck does more than observe; he diagnoses. The "hatred of aliens"—whether migrants, Jews, Muslims, or the racially 'othered'—has always been the scapegoat of weakened empires. The "wounded manhood" refers to the fragility of patriarchal power, of leaders and followers desperate to recover a mythic past. And "the frailty of power"— a phrase that captures both its intoxicating illusion and its ultimate impotence—reminds us how quickly confidence crumbles into chaos.

Clash of Civilizations: The Rejected and Despised

As Peck speaks, more images of Hitler flash across the screen. The masses cheer. The narrative warns, but the visuals remember. Then, abruptly, the screen fades to a very different scene: a vast, desolate landscape. The camera hovers over what appears to be an abandoned oil field. The desert stretches in every direction, lifeless and windswept. Rusted machinery lies in ruin—left behind after extraction. It is likely the Middle East. Or perhaps another exploited land, emptied of resources, robbed of sovereignty.

Raoul narrates: "The Western world is panicking—a delirious, spiraling panic, complaining about a clash of civilizations, thus displaying the limits of superiority." This reference to the so-called "clash of civilizations" theory, popularized by political scientist Samuel P. Huntington in the 1990s, is not incidental. The theory posited that future global conflict would be cultural, especially between the West and the Islamic world. It became a self-fulfilling prophecy—justifying wars, drone strikes, and surveillance while ignoring the colonial histories and violent economic policies that caused the instability in the first place.

Peck continues: "Privilege makes you vulnerable. And panic, when blended with ignorance and bigotry, creates anger—limitless and blinding anger." That anger now defines political life in much of the Western world: not directed upward, at the true architects of exploitation, but downward—at the refugee, the migrant, the foreigner. History repeats not as farce, but as fury. "Everyone else becomes the enemy. The fortress becomes a prison. Everyone else looking in at you."

Now the screen shows the brutal cost of these panicked, exclusionary policies. Homeless immigrants huddle in makeshift shelters, tents made from tarps and discarded sheets. They are not invaders—they are survivors. Women holding infants, teenagers with hollow eyes, families seeking warmth beneath plastic. Another cut: young immigrant men detained in local jails or border holding areas. Their faces reflect trauma and waiting. For some, the holding area will become a deportation cell.

These are people whose homelands have been devastated by imperialism and its lasting effects, now seeking a better life in countries that offer hope. But, yet, they are rejected and despised by many. The truth is too plain to ignore. From Latin America to West Africa to the Middle East, the same pattern plays out: Western empires take, destroy, and then build walls to keep out the human consequences of their own betrayal, exploitation, and violence.

The people who now knock at the gates once served as the labor force, the resource base, the test subjects, the colonies. Their stories are bound to the fortunes of the very nations now rejecting them. And this rejection is not new—it is simply more visible.

The image on the screen now shows a vast sea—endless, gray, indifferent. Its surface churns with both beauty and threat. Upon its waves, rescue rafts drift, packed tightly with black migrants who have risked everything to cross. No navy protects them. In some cases, no coast welcomes them. These are the displaced, the desperate, the human collateral of wars, famines, and economic policies that began with imperialism, planned in boardrooms and ended in loss, desperation and blood.

One close-up (actual footage) reveals the face of a woman whose face is troubled with tears flowing from her eyes. Raoul Peck narrates: "People die because they are hungry and can't protect their own existence. Others because they are persecuted, or because they can't feed themselves, protect themselves, or care for their children."

The narration does not dramatize—it testifies. These are not isolated tragedies; they are systemic consequences. People flee because the conditions at home have become unlivable, and often those conditions were engineered or exploited by foreign powers who now shut the gates behind them.

As Peck's words continue, the images shift: immigrants walking through the desert. The sun is merciless. They carry children on their shoulders, bags in their hands, and nothing left but resolve. Another image appears: a small family sitting on a bench with all they own—suitcases packed, children curled up asleep. It is the portrait of exhaustion and helplessness. A snapshot of lives in limbo. They are not criminals, not invaders, not threats. They are the desperate poor—made poor by systems too vast and too cruel to name in a soundbite.

Then, in an abrupt and jarring cut, the screen flashes to a video image— clean, high-resolution, posed. It is the 2019 G20 Summit in Osaka. Thirty-eight world leaders stand shoulder to shoulder, dressed in tailored suits. The contrast could not be sharper. These are the architects of policy, the inheritors of empire, the arbiters of global wealth—and they do not look tired. They do not look exiled.

Peck continues his narration: "Meanwhile, the pornographic rich are the new moralists." The phrase pierces. "These are not simply the wealthy, they are the pornographically rich: so obscenely, indecently bloated with wealth that it shatters any illusion of fairness. And yet, they preach to the world. They publish books on leadership. They lecture the poor about "resilience."

They manufacture TED Talks on "vision" while offshore accounts drain nations of their futures. "Most disturbing is not the images or even the terrifying words." "Most disturbing here is the absence of ridicule, and the silence of complacency."

That silence is everywhere. It's in the parliaments that approve new border walls. It's in the press that calls the drowning "migrants" instead of people. It's in the middle-class comfort that looks away, too embarrassed to stare, too afraid to act. "Any hint of decency has definitely been lost in the picture."

The documentary does not need to raise its voice. It shows us the picture—and the picture indicts us. The same sea that carried empire's ships now swallows those it dispossessed. The same nations that drew borders now militarize them. The same leaders who toast at summits also sign the sanctions, approve the bombings, and then offer platitudes about "shared values." *There is no irony left. Only clarity.*

Appearing on the screen is the caption: Murder in Pacot, Raoul Peck, 2014. The name "Pacot" refers to a district located in the hills above Port-au-Prince, Haiti. This neighborhood—Pétion-Ville—once represented wealth, colonial privilege, and the gated optimism of Haiti's elite. But following the devastating 2010 earthquake, many of these walled enclaves crumbled, revealing not only the instability of concrete but the fragility of class illusions.

Raoul Peck's 2014 film Murder in Pacot uses this physical and metaphorical collapse to examine post-disaster inequality, exploitation, and the historical contradictions of Haitian identity in the shadow of colonial and neocolonial power. It is against this haunting backdrop—

where homes become ruins and silence hides trauma—that Peck sets this section of the documentary.

Raoul begins to narrate: "We search for truth when we should search for meaning." The screen shows a video of young adult Haitians dancing—dancing not just as expression, but as survival, as cultural defiance, as embodied memory. This is joy resisting despair. Life asserting itself against the architecture of devastation. The camera doesn't merely capture movement—it captures a people refusing to be erased.

Peck repeats: "We search for truth when we should search for meaning." The very existence of this film, he tells us, is a miracle. The narrative then jolts the viewer with a haunting story: a reference to an 18-year-old Palestinian girl, strapped with explosives, who detonates herself in a crowd at a discotheque in Tel Aviv. The screen does not sensationalize the act—it questions its genesis. Peck reflects with painful introspection: "When others think about revenge, I think about my daughter. What would have pushed her to commit such a horrific act? Would I call my child a monster?" He answers himself, haltingly, with a haunting refrain: "Yes… It is complicated."

Peck's Tribute to Sven

A black-and-white image of a desolate desert appears—dry, empty, lifeless. The land speaks in silence. Raoul narrates: "Today I learned of Sven's death. It wasn't sudden. I knew it would happen soon. I had learned to cope. It's not pain that I feel, but rage and sorrow."

Now we see images of Sven Von Storch, Peck's close friend and collaborator—an intellectual and a believer in stories that unsettle and speak truth to power. "Sven gave me the original impulse for this story," Peck continues, "and he washed away my doubts that such a film was even conceivable. Up until this day, he wanted it to happen. Finishing this story is now vital."

The documentary lingers on the vast desert again, this time accompanied by an image of Sven—his face soft with thought, his legacy preserved through testimony and vision. Then the camera lifts to a wide shot of dense woodlands, a canopy of life unfolding in emerald waves. The view transitions smoothly to reveal, from a bird's-eye perspective, a sprawling city emerging in the distance—skyscrapers, roads, the heartbeat of industry. Then comes another city, this one aglow at night, bathed in electric light and the quiet hum of modernity.

Renewal and Calling to Account

Peck's voice returns: "Nobody starts with a clean slate. But the human condition also requires that the practice of power and domination be renewed. It is that renewal that should concern us most. Calling to account the so-called legacies of past horrors—slavery, colonialism, or the Holocaust—is only possible because of that renewal."

And that renewal, he warns, does not reside in textbooks, monuments, or speeches—it occurs only in the present. "Only in that present," Peck says, "can we be true or false to the past we choose to acknowledge."

And with that, he echoes the words of Haitian historian Michel-Rolph Trouillot: "The facts are staring us in the face. Time is not a chronological continuity... it is the range of disjointed moments, practices, and symbols that thread the historical relations between events and narratives."

A new video segment appears. We are no longer in the wilderness or among the ruins, but on a televised stage—studio lights beaming, polished words polished for performance. A panel of seven people sits in discussion. The moderator, Christine Amanpour, holds the space. The program is titled ABC This Week. The caption that flashes boldly across the screen is jarring: HOLY WAR. Subtext follows like a challenge: Should Americans fear Islam? Then, beneath that, the words: Moderates vs. Extremists.

Peck captures the shifting expressions of the audience—uncertainty, intensity, confusion, suspicion. In this next montage, we are ushered into the chaotic swirl of public discourse. Clip after clip reveals everyday people, journalists, and pundits reflecting—or rather reacting—to the theme of Holy War. One person admits plainly: "You know, I'm not an expert in religion." Another voice, drawn from a different studio, announces, "This is a hardline issue for people who live in border states." The tone is not of understanding but of position-staking. A third commentator warns, "The President is trying to protect our borders from an invasion."

Then comes a strangely misplaced voice—Dr. Phil. "Forty-five thousand people a year die from automobile accidents," he comments. The absurd juxtaposition is part of Peck's point. Rational comparisons dissolve into soundbites. Context is sacrificed on the altar of opinion.

Peck's narration returns with pointed gravity: "American scholars have largely abandoned the role of public intellectuals to pundits and entertainers." And so, knowledge becomes noise. Conviction becomes combat. In a flickering instant, another scene unfolds: Fox News: The Kelly File. A panel discusses race in America. The exchange is manicured, but beneath the civility lies rage and evasion.

Peck cuts in: "No proof, no arguments are necessary. It is opinions against opinions, shamelessly passing off impotence as reason." And then he lands the blow: "We now know that narratives are made of silences." Silences that birth myths. Silences that cover blood.

CHAPTER 14

White Man's Neighborhood - Keep Out

As the voices of the present drone on, the documentary pivots, pulling us backward into the cold, deliberate silence of history. A black-and-white photograph comes into view. It is the year 1920. The image: Charles Davenport, the biologist known as the father of American eugenics. Peck's voice is steady and unflinching: "This man was the leader of the American eugenics movement." We are told that Davenport asks his friend Madison Grant, author of The Passing of the Great Race. "Can we build a wall high enough around this country so as to keep out those cheaper races?"

The year changes—May 26, 1924. President Calvin Coolidge signs the Johnson-Reed Immigration Act into law. A restriction act. A wall not of brick, but of policy. "It shut down immigration by 97%," Peck explains. "The doors were shut for 40 years. People tend to forget."

A victory. But for whom? "A political victory for eugenics," Peck says.

The documentary's images switch. A long, stretching contemporary border wall is in view. Then, a different kind of wall—on a home window hangs a sign: Japs, Keep Out. Then a larger sign: Japs Keep Moving. This is a White Man's Neighborhood.

The montage grows heavier. Drawings now appear—cartoonish yet menacing. Angry white men scowl, their hats labeled with words once used to justify exclusion: Outlaw. Criminal. Degenerate. Mafia. Illiterate. Pauper. Antichrist. Peck continues, unwavering: "A political victory for eugenics. As one congressman said, the nation would remain the home of a great people. Christian, English-speaking, white people."

Then the image widens. The crowd of angry cartoon men swells. At their center stands Uncle Sam, draped in red, white, and blue. He holds an olive branch and waves the American flag. The flag says "Liberty"—but behind it, engraved on stone, are the words: DANGER TO AMERICAN IDEAS AND INSTITUTIONS.

We must ask: What liberty? Whose liberty? Whose ideas are protected, and whose are destroyed?

Peck offers this narration: "The open arms of Ellis Island are now closed again." The symbolic gateway to America's immigrant story—the very promise etched at the base of the Statue of Liberty—had been sealed shut, not just by policy but by fear, racism, and nationalism disguised as security. The law closed the doors on Jews who were fleeing the Nazis. For the lack of a visa, Anne Frank died in Bergen-Belsen concentration camp." The image of a non-white child now haunts the screen.

Next, the screen flashes a somber catalog of consequences in stark red letters: Aftermath, Cultural Losses, Dislocation, Moral Deterioration, Political Changes. These are not abstractions; they are the scars left behind when a world closes its eyes, its borders, and its conscience.

"Adolf's Racial Paradise"

A black-and-white aerial image appears. A plane flies over a city. It carried Adolf Hitler. The screen reads: Adolf's Racial Paradise. Raoul narrates: "When Adolf Hitler entered politics, the opportunities for Germany to expand had been closed. He had to find an alternative, closer to home." This was not merely a strategy of conquest—it was a colonial impulse reborn in Europe's own backyard. Hitler's campaign to the East was, in effect, his own version of imperial expansion—a colonial war, mirroring the methods and ideologies once deployed by Western empires abroad.

The screen now displays a map: Hungary, Berlin, Eastern Prussia, and neighboring territories. Peck continues, "The Lebensraum—meaning living space—according to Hitler's imperial vision, found its precedent not in European tradition but in American practice. The elimination of 'America's redskins,' as Hitler crudely referred to Native Americans, was the perfect example of successful colonization."

Here, Peck draws a chilling connection: what the U.S. had done to its Indigenous population—through removal, starvation, warfare, and the erasure of their societies—became a blueprint. Video footage now shows grainy, black-and-white clips of the Nazi regime expanding into Czechoslovakia, Poland, and beyond. The marching boots, the raised flags, the seized streets—each frame echoes a past we have not fully reckoned with.

Raoul resumes: "Like the Americans had done, he would proceed to send German settlers to replace all Jewish and Slavic populations in the East." This was not incidental; it was programmatic. The law of blood justified both the needs and the deeds. Hitler's anti-Semitism—ferocious and fanatical—was not an aberration in history. It was rooted in centuries of

European religious and racial hatred, codified in church councils, ghettos, expulsions, and massacres long before the 20th century.

Genocidal Liquidation

Appearing on screen: Kovno, Lithuania, 1941. Then: Pogrom in Zloczow, now Ukraine, 1941. The images are raw and unflinching. Jews and other non-Aryan civilians are brutally beaten, some already slain, others forced to lie down before being executed in the streets. The piles of bodies are not metaphors—they are indictments.

Peck narrates: "But the step from mass murder to genocide was not taken until the anti-Semitic tradition met the tradition of genocide that rose during Europe's expansion in America, Australia, Africa, and Asia." The industrial efficiency of death—the gas chambers, the bureaucratic lists, the train schedules—was only possible once the ideological framework had been *normalized*. Western colonization had already supplied the pattern: the dehumanization of an entire people, the notion of racial hierarchy, and the use of violence as a tool of order.

Raoul continues: "According to Lebensraum theory, the Jews belong to an even lower race than the Russians and the Poles—a race which could not lay claim to the right to live." Appearing now on screen are the haunting words: Liquidation of the Mizocz Ghetto, now Ukraine, 1942. A new image follows—dozens of naked and barely clothed women and children being murdered by two Nazi soldiers. Their bodies lie limp, stripped of dignity, of humanity, of life itself.

Peck continues: "It was only natural," in Hitler's twisted calculus, "that such lower races should be exterminated if they were in the way." He notes: "The other Western master race had done just that." The United States. Belgium. Britain. Spain. "Same procedures apply. Different players."

On screen now: Warsaw Ghetto, Poland, 1942. Jews, with hands raised in terror, cower before armed Nazi soldiers. Then appear the images of naked corpses—emaciated, dumped like refuse into mass graves. Peck's voice lingers on one grim truth: "They died on their own—when the food supply was cut off." Another method in the machine of genocide

The sad rule that so-called inferior people died out upon contact with highly cultivated people was at work again." This perverse logic—that contact with civilization justifies extinction—was not new. It had already been applied to Native Americans, Aboriginal Australians, Congolese, Herero, and Nama peoples. Now it was being turned inward, on the European continent itself.

And we must ask again: *What liberty? Whose liberty? Whose ideas are protected, and whose are destroyed?*

Appearing on the screen are the words: Deportation from Westerbork Camp, Netherlands to Poland, 1944.

Westerbork, originally constructed in 1939 as a refugee camp for Jews fleeing Nazi Germany, was turned by the German occupiers into a transit hub in 1942. From there, over 100,000 Dutch Jews, including Anne Frank and her family, were deported to extermination camps—primarily Auschwitz and Sobibor. These so-called "deportations" were, in fact, death sentences, cloaked in bureaucratic language and efficient train schedules.

Images now appear of countless Jews being escorted to railway cars—human cargo, packed into cattle wagons without food, water, or the faintest hope of return. There are before images, capturing the cramped and desolate conditions at the train stations, the desperation and confusion on the faces of those about to be taken. These are followed by after-images—present-day photos of the same locations—empty, barren, and haunted by silence. Concrete still remembers what history tries to forget.

Raoul Peck narrates: "A Nazi officer took these pictures. Like the previous ones, they were found in what has come to be called The Auschwitz Album—the accounting of death." This album is the only known photographic evidence of the arrival and processing of Jews at Auschwitz-Birkenau, taken by SS officers themselves in 1944. It captures faces, bodies, and moments frozen at the threshold of genocide. These images were never meant to be seen by the world—they were private trophies of horror. The Auschwitz Album, discovered after the war by a survivor, became an essential document of what the Nazis tried to hide.

Peck continues: "Beneath the numbers, there are faces. There are souls—caught for one small moment by the lens of their tormentors. And they know. They must have known." One image shows a woman's face—exhausted, resigned, yet still piercing the camera with unmistakable humanity. Her gaze, almost too alive, too aware, defies erasure.

20 Minute Walk of Death: "The Banality of Evil"

"Unfit to work." That was the Nazi classification for those condemned immediately upon arrival: children, the elderly, the sick, pregnant women. "Selection" was the euphemism—life or death determined in seconds by an officer's gesture to the right or to the left. This group, Peck narrates, "is saved momentarily. A mother, a child, an aunt—walking through the motion of hope, walking towards what they were told was water." "Where can we have water the children ask. "Walk all the way to the back. There is water, I promise, says the SS officer."

And so they walk towards Crematoriums 4 and 5, located at the far end of Birkenau. These crematoriums—equipped with gas chambers disguised as showers—were engineered for mass murder. Up to 2,000 people at a time could be killed in one gassing. Zyklon B, a cyanide-based pesticide, was dropped from overhead vents. Within 20 minutes, all would be dead.

Raoul continues: "20 minutes. That's the time it takes to get from the dock, across the tracks, along the stony path, all the way to the back of the camp." Twenty minutes to walk into oblivion. In total, over 1.1 million people were murdered at Auschwitz, most of them Jews, but also Roma, Poles, Soviet POWs, and others deemed "undesirable." As the Soviet Red Army approached in January 1945, the SS attempted to destroy the evidence. They blew up Crematoriums II, III, IV, and V. But enough remains—bricks, twisted metal, records, and most of all, testimonies—to bear witness.

The ground still tells the truth, even when textbooks and politics refuse to.

These images, and Peck's unrelenting narration, force us to confront what Hannah Arendt once called "the banality of evil"—a bureaucratic, routinized, industrial-scale genocide carried out not by monsters alone, but by ordinary men in uniforms, by clerks, chemists, train conductors, and soldiers who followed orders without question.

The Holocaust was not an accident. It was a deliberate policy—rooted in racial ideology, sanctioned by law, implemented with precision, and accepted by a complicit society. And the machinery of that genocide, from the paperwork to the poison gas, bears chilling resemblance to other moments in modern history when fear, race, and empire intersected with lethal consequences.

And we must ask again, as Peck's documentary demands: *What liberty? Whose liberty? Whose ideas are protected, and whose are destroyed?*

The camera now drifts across a vast ocean. A Nazi naval ship is navigating the water. Onboard, officers laugh, joke, and drink in leisure; some of the officers are accompanied by family members. They are at ease. This is not the picture many imagine when they think of war criminals. This is not a battlefield—this is a cruise. And yet, they are architects of genocide.

Not Ignorant Brutes

Raoul Peck's voice slices through the calm: "It's time to own up to a basic truth." The great planners and executioners of the Final Solution were not ignorant brutes. No, they were men of stature. Men of titles. They held university degrees—many from the most prestigious European institutions. Some had PhDs. They were philosophers, engineers, artists, scientists. This was an elite, not of conscience, but of coordination. This was evil forged not in the dark corners of ignorance, but in the fluorescent-lit halls of bureaucracy and scholarship.

The documentary now shows images of Germans—enthusiastic Nazi supporters—dancing, smiling, parading on the deck of a luxury vessel. It is a Nazi leisure cruise, a floating symbol of racial triumph and Aryan joy.

The same hands that designed gas chambers clink glasses in celebration. Soldiers puff cigars and pipes alongside Adolf Hitler himself. This is not incidental. This is intentional. Nazi Germany did not operate in secret. It was a national mobilization. Total war included total society.

Peck continues: "All German production capabilities were mobilized to create this racial paradise." The term Volksgemeinschaft—the people's community—was the ideological glue. It summoned the talents of architects to design death camps. It summoned plumbers to install the pipes for the gas chambers. It summoned manufacturers to build ovens and banks to manage stolen wealth. Landscapers mapped the grounds for aesthetic death. Agronomists studied how to grow food for some while orchestrating starvation for others. SS henchmen merely stood at the end of a long chain of willing collaborators. The organizational efficiency was unparalleled, chilling in its precision.

Crematorium Blueprint - A Killing Machine

Now appears on the screen a detailed drawing: Cross-Section of Crematorium III by David Olère, a Jewish-French painter, a former prisoner at Auschwitz-Birkenau. He survived the hell he painted. His work bears witness. His rendering shows that this killing machine was no accident. It was constructed with deliberate sophistication. Each section of the crematorium blueprint is labeled:

- Section A: The Undressing Room—where victims were told to disrobe, often under the lie that they were going to be disinfected.
- Section B: The Holding Cell—an antechamber of death, where people waited unknowingly for the poison.

- Section C: The Mechanical Lift for the Corpses—designed to maximize efficiency, transporting the dead like factory products.

- Section D: The Gas Chamber—itself disguised to look like a shower, complete with false showerheads.

- Section E: The Grate for the Gas Canister—where Zyklon B was dropped in.

- Section F: SS Experimental Dissection Room—where bodies were cut open in the name of pseudoscience.

- Section G: SS Entry Corridor—a protected passage for officers to observe without risk.

- Section H: The Incineration Ovens—where the dead were reduced to ash.

- Section I: Coal Wagon on Rails—for feeding the flames.

And so on—down to Section Q—each segment a cold, clinical part of a system built for mass death.

"We Still Haven't Seen Anything Yet"

Suddenly, the scene changes. The "white man" on his motorcycle is shown again, riding through a hilly terrain, surrounded by nothingness. Wyclef Jean sings "Knockin' on Heaven's Door." The tone is mournful, almost prophetic. The rider crashes. His motorcycle skids and falls. He tries to lift it, but cannot. In frustration, he kicks it and stumbles. The desert, like history, has turned against him.

As he gathers himself, he sees figures approaching—Black people, emerging from the tree line. Among them is a pregnant woman. The camera slows. They look at him. He looks at them. Suspicion. Memory. Reckoning.

The "white man" panics. He turns and begins to run—uphill, panting, scrambling. He flees not from an act of violence but from the weight of history. He flees from those whose stories his world tried to erase. He stops, breathless, turns back—and there they are, still watching. One of them holds a stone.

Old images now appear in black and white: A European man flanks a European woman as they read the newspaper. Then, more dated images of Europeans people watching a black and white television scene; modern images are then provided of people viewing their devices and computers. Superimposed on the screen are the words: "It's not knowledge we lack."

Raoul resumes his voiceover: "It's not knowledge we lack. Just as educated Frenchmen in the 1950s and 1960s knew what their troops were doing in Vietnam and Algeria. Just as educated Russians in the 1980s knew what their soldiers did in Afghanistan. Just as educated South Africans and Americans during that same period knew what their auxiliaries were doing in Mozambique and Central America, respectively."

This is not an indictment of ignorance—it is an indictment of knowing and doing nothing. It is an indictment of polite complicity. Peck continues: "So too, educated Europeans today know how children die when the whip of debt and bombs whistle over poor countries."

The screen flashes images of a garbage heap, death camps, destruction from war and a forest set ablaze. These are not the past. These are the present. And Peck reminds us that Auschwitz was not a freak occurrence—it was merely the industrial application of ancient systems of extermination: Colonialism. Slavery. Pogroms. Theologies of conquest. Capitalism without conscience. Socialism without soul. Democracy without the demos.

"The educated general public has always largely known what atrocities have been committed and are being committed in the name of progress, civilization, socialism, democracy, and the market." Peck reminds us, this has been true for a thousand years—since the original Christian crusades. Since Christendom's violent baptism of Europe and the sacking of Jerusalem.

"No, it is not knowledge that is lacking."

It has always been preserved. It can be found in archives, in photographs, in memories, in ruins, and even in language. In scholarly language, as when European imperialists wrote with cold certainty: "Imperialism is a biologically necessary process that, according to the law of nature, leads to the inevitable destruction of the lower race." And so Peck makes it plain: It is not that we didn't know. It is that we knew—and did not care.

The documentary returns to the white man's desperate flight. He is no longer sprinting out of fear. The camera shows him on the crest of a hill, where his hands tremble around a large hunting knife. Without hesitation, he drops to his knees and begins stabbing the blade into the ground, digging frantically. Each thrust is a mix of panic and muscle memory, as though he has done this before—buried something for just such a day as this.

The earth gives way slowly, stubbornly, but fear lends him strength. His eyes keep darting toward the tree line below, the place where they had first appeared. At last, the knife strikes his treasure. He claws at the soil until a small cache is revealed: weapons—tools of destruction he once trusted. He pulls them free and inspects them quickly. One by one, his face hardens with disbelief and dread. None of them works. The steel is rusted, the triggers jammed, the powder spoiled. In his moment of greatest need, his instruments of domination have betrayed him.

Then movement—a blur—erupts from the corner of the frame. One of the Black pursuers crashes into him, and instinct takes over. The white man's arm flashes, the knife drives deep, and the first attacker collapses, lifeless.

From the trees, two more emerge. The "white man" draws his sidearm in a single motion, fires twice. Both fall before they can close the distance. He stands, chest heaving, gun still hot in his hand.

But there is no time to breathe. A fourth man bursts from the wood line with a wordless cry, tackling him to the ground. They roll in the dirt, limbs locked in a brutal contest. The" white man" manages to twist, forcing his opponent beneath him. Then both his hands are at the man's throat, squeezing with relentless fury. The Black man's struggles weaken, then cease.

The camera pulls back—slowly, inexorably—revealing a wider and wider circle of figures emerging from the woods. Dozens of Black men and women, silent but advancing, surrounding the lone figure still hunched over the man he has just killed. It is a tableau of inevitability.

Suddenly—cut, the scene changes! The white man bolts upright, gasping. Sweat glistens on his skin. The weapons, the struggle, the encirclement—all of it was a dream, a nightmare born of fear and memory.

Now he is back in the dim hut, the air thick with the scent of damp earth. It is the same hut where the Black woman had once, with contempt, bathed him. She stands over him now, eyes unblinking, a gun leveled at his head, a reversal of the multiple images showing the "white man" displaying and initiating his deadly authority.

His gaze flicks toward his own firearm lying nearby. His hand twitches toward it, but stops. They both know the truth—he will never reach it before the woman pulls the trigger. They stare at each other in a tense, frozen moment that holds the weight of centuries.

Without warning, the film shifts again. We are with a different white man now—Captain Willard, who is presented in Coppola's movie as follows. Superimposed on the screen are the words: Apocalypse Now, Francis Ford Coppola, 1979. The song of Elmore James's The Sky Is Crying begins to play.

In this footage, the modern depiction of Captain Willard is presented—half-naked, unshaven, spiraling, alone in a dimly lit hotel room. He is no longer the distant soldier sent on a mission in Vietnam—he is now every man undone by the violence of empire. A man possessed by his own demons.

He stares into a mirror, perhaps hoping to recognize himself again. But there's nothing there. Suddenly, in a fit of despair and rage, he strikes the mirror with his bare hand, shattering the reflection and slicing open his skin. Blood runs freely down his arm. He stares at his hands, now soaked in red, and rubs them together. Then, in an act of desperate self-absolution—or condemnation—he smears the blood across his face.

The symbolism is unmistakable: he is both executioner and scapegoat. He reaches for a bottle of liquor and begins to drink greedily, trying to silence the cries of the innocent and the judgment of his own conscience. It is a futile ritual. The bottle cannot cleanse his soul.

Raoul Peck begins to narrate: "Everywhere in the world, where knowledge is being suppressed—Knowledge that, if it were made known, would shatter our image of the world and force us to question ourselves—Everywhere there, Heart of Darkness is being enacted."

Here, Peck deliberately references Joseph Conrad's infamous novella, a work that laid bare the moral rot at the heart of European imperialism. In "Heart of Darkness," it was the Belgian Congo. In "Apocalypse Now," it was Vietnam. But in Peck's telling, it is everywhere—it is the United States, the Caribbean, Africa, Palestine, Haiti, and beyond. Wherever the history of white domination has gone unexamined or sanitized, there the darkness festers.

The screen then shifts to the image of Seminole leader Abby Osceola, executed earlier in the documentary by General Thomas Jesup—the same Jesup who has been shown throughout the film as the archetype of the "white man." Osceola's murder by deception, while under a flag of truce, remains one of the most dishonorable moments in American military history. Following Osceola's image, a slow montage of black and white photographs of Native Americans appears.

Raoul returns with narration, quoting the sacred lament of Black Elk, the Oglala Lakota holy man: "After the Wounded Knee Massacre, I didn't know then how much was ended. When I look back now from this hill of old age, I can still see the butchered women and children lying heaped and scattered all along the crooked gulch as plain as when I saw them with eyes still young. And I can see that something else died there, in the bloody mud, and was buried in the blizzard. A people's dream died there. It was a beautiful dream. The nation's circle is broken and scattered. There is no center any longer. And the sacred tree is dead."

Peck repeats, with aching clarity: *"A people's dream died there."*

As the documentary approaches its closing sequence, the screen circles back to the dramatized massacre from the Seminole War of 1836. The audience sees the lifeless bodies of Native Americans and African Maroons—freedom fighters, not slaves—lying on the ground, strewn across the battlefield in a grotesque ballet of slaughter.

This re-enactment exposes what is often hidden: that the Seminole Wars were not mere frontier skirmishes, but full-scale efforts to annihilate both Indigenous sovereignty and Black liberation. The Maroons who lived among the Seminoles were descendants of escaped slaves, and their alliance posed a direct threat to the Southern slave economy. The U.S. government's answer was total war.

General Jesup, the "white man" standing in the midst of the carnage he helped unleash, walks the field, watching as flames engulf bodies and smoke blots out the sun. His breathing is labored; his steps unsteady. He begins to remove his garments—his coat, his sash, his uniform, discarding the symbols of his identity. In silence, he walks into a nearby pond. As he moves deeper into the water, the camera begins flashing images—visions of massacre, of conquest, of empire. A hut burns in a distant land. The bodies of children lie limp in the mud. Snapshots of horror flash like memories—perhaps his, perhaps ours.

Standing neck-deep in the water, Jesup slowly lowers himself beneath the surface. It is a suicide, yes—but also a symbolic baptism into the guilt of white Western civilization. A civilization that once called itself the light of the world, but left behind only ruin.

The screen abruptly cuts to the site of another graveyard of history: Auschwitz II-Birkenau. The name appears superimposed across the screen. The camera slowly pans the vast expanse of the concentration camp—barracks, gates, barbed wire. No actors. No music. Just a place where evil made itself a system.

In the distance, voices rise—not in fear, but in defiant protest. Chants can be heard, growing louder: No justice, no peace! Do not let our planet die! Do not let our planet die!

Then the voice of Greta Thunberg emerges—not as a politician, but as a prophet of this generation: "We still haven't seen anything yet. This is only the beginning of the beginning."

More chants fill the air: We are all together. We are all here. As the camera continues its wide, solemn scan of Auschwitz II, a somber, pensive melody plays. Finally, Raoul Peck offers one last piercing observation: "No, it's not knowledge we lack."

The screen fades to black. The documentary ends—not with closure, but with confrontation. Not with answers, but with a haunting question:

What will we now do with what we know?